THE
BIG
RETIREMENT LIE

THE
BIG
RETIREMENT LIE

WHY TRADITIONAL RETIREMENT PLANNING BENEFITS THE IRS MORE THAN YOU

MICHAEL D. REESE
CFP®, CLU, CHFC

COPPER LEAF
PUBLISHING

Traverse City, Michigan

Published by Copper Leaf Publishing
Traverse City, MI

Publisher's Cataloging-in-Publication Data
Reese, Michael D.

The big retirement lie : why traditional retirement planning benefits the IRS more than you / Michael D. Reese.—Traverse City, MI : Copper Leaf Pub., 2007.

p. ; cm.
ISBN: 978-0-9795517-0-3

1. Retirement—United States—Planning. 2. Retirement. 3. Internal Revenue Service. I. Title.

HQ1063.2.U6 R44 2007
649.79—dc22 2007934425

Project production and coordination by Jenkins Group, Inc
www.BookPublishing.com

Printed in the United States of America
11 10 09 08 07 • 5 4 3 2

Contents

Foreword

For some, the phrase, "Perfect Storm," is becoming overused. But there likely exists no better phrase for what's happening in America right now when it comes to retirement planning. Four powerful forces, each one troublesome on its own, are coming together to create the Perfect Storm that could have a drastic impact across the retirement landscape as we know it today.

First, we encounter the rapid decline of the traditional pension plan. In 1985, 112,000 American corporations provided a pension plan for its employees. This created a solid foundation for a retiree, knowing that they had a guaranteed income that could be relied upon, no matter how long they should live.* Just 20 years later, in 2005, 70% of those plans vanished into thin air.* By 2005, less than 32,000 companies still offered a pension plan, and the number is shrinking every year.*

Fewer & fewer companies provide a pension plan anymore. Instead, many have replaced the traditional pension with a 401(k). They used to fund your pension, now you primarily fund your 401(k).

Second, we encounter the staggering growth of healthcare costs. If healthcare costs just grew at the rate of inflation, it would not be nearly as big a problem. However, the costs of healthcare are

*Source: Journal of Financial Planning, April 2005

increasing at a rate well beyond that of inflation, and have been for many years.

In 1950, healthcare costs represented approximately 4% of the average American household budget.** By 2004, that percentage has skyrocketed to 17%! And it's not getting better anytime soon.**

Third, we find the National Debt at an all-time high. As of April 2005, it's now close to $7.5 trillion and getting larger every year.*** In order to give this number some perspective, think about it this way. If every household in America had to pony up enough money to pay off the National Debt, we would have to come up with approximately $450,000 each. That's right—$450,000 per household!

So far, what do we have? Government is spending more and more of our money, and what's happening to the population at the same time? It's getting older, isn't it? We have what is referred to as the "Graying of America". More people are retiring, and we have fewer workers, yet what is government doing? Spending more money!

What do you think will happen to the tax code pretty soon? Doesn't it seem likely that at some point somebody's got to clean up the mess and pay the bill?

That brings me to the fourth, and final force, that's leading to the Perfect Storm. More & more retirement dollars being held by Americans are found in tax-deferred accounts. That means that every single dollar will be taxed as it's extracted from these accounts. So guess who's likely to end up paying for most of these costs? Maybe you and your retirement accounts?

**Source: Bureau of Economic Analysis, printed in *Investors Business Daily*, 1/25/05
***Source: Bureau of the Public Debt, 2005

The good news is that every cloud comes with a silver lining. Today, that silver lining is often found in retirement planning opportunities.

We are currently sitting on historically low tax rates. You have the opportunity to take advantage of planning right now to improve your future, and the cost to do so is at an all-time low! You may never again have the opportunity that you have right now to take advantage of the many retirement planning opportunities that exists today. A number of which are discussed in this book. I would encourage you to sit down with an experienced financial services professional to explore and learn how these opportunities could specifically affect you.

It's been said that those who fail to plan, plan to fail. If you hide your head in the sand, you may be swept away in the Perfect Storm. If you keep your eyes open, however, you likely have a brief window in which you can take advantage of the opportunity to sail towards calmer waters. If you chart your course today with purpose and knowledge, you can avoid the Perfect Storm.

Brent D. Enders
President, USA Financial®

Affiliates by common ownership:
USA Financial Marketing™—Advisor Advancement—
    Wholesale Insurance Distribution
USA Financial Securities™— Member NASD/SIPC—
    Registered Investment Advisor
USA Financial Formulas™—Formulaic Investing™ Strategies—
    Registered Investment Advisor

Acknowledgments

This book was born at a charity auction in the winter of 2003. And my wife, Becky, is 100 percent responsible.

Like many husbands, I sometimes think that I know a bit more than the "average guy." And I used to talk about how "someday" I was going to write a book. Well, you know how "someday" never seems to come.

So there we were, sitting at the auction table, and up comes a "Book Publishing Package" for bid. Without bothering to consult me, Becky decided (all on her own) that it was time for me to put my money where my mouth was. Next thing I know, she is bidding away on this book publishing package.

I tried to stop her. I tried to tell her that I was just kidding about writing a book. I'm no author! But she didn't seem to hear me, which is surprising, as she always claims that I'm the one with selective hearing.

So she ends up winning this book publishing package, and then all I had to do was write my book, the publishing was already "paid for." But it turned out that actually writing a book is easier said than done. Getting my thoughts down on paper was hard!

Fast forward to the beginning of November 2006. Becky and I were at a meeting where someone else had written a book. It was about 100 pages long, and he was talking about how easy it was for him to do. Becky gave me a nudge, and I opened my big mouth. (I'm a guy, so you know that this is probably not going to be a good idea!)

I actually claimed that I was "working" on a book myself, and that it should be done by the end of the year. And I didn't stop there. I told the group that they should expect to have a copy by our next meeting in March. (Yep, sometimes I wonder about myself, too.)

I hadn't written one page (that I kept) and I just gave myself a very public deadline of two months to get this thing done. Did Becky tell me that I was an idiot? You bet she did! But she also supported me 100 percent.

This book is being wrapped up in mid-February 2007, so I missed my deadline, but it's done. For three-and-a-half months, Becky and my five children have supported my efforts. A couple of the kids have even been running around bragging about how Daddy is an "author." I'm convinced that they're not really sure what it means, but I'll take it.

I want to give special thanks to Sherry Tucker, who has helped me step-by-step get this book done. I also want to thank my co-workers, Jon Torbet, Chris Davis, and Erica Veliquette, for their steadfast support. And a special thanks also goes out to Jim Casler, who helped make this book better than it would have been otherwise.

Of course, my deepest gratitude goes out to my wife, Becky, for her support, and to my five children: Sara, Taylor, Brendan, Morgan, and Madison. Becky, thank you for everything you do.

Preface

"If everyone was right, we'd all be rich and happy!"
—Unknown

Isn't the world of financial advice filled with contradicting opinions? Just turn on one of the financial news shows, and you can find two "experts" going at each other, on opposites sides of the fence, both armed with piles of charts and data to prove their point.

But there is one thing that they all agree on. Everyone agrees that when it comes to retirement planning, you should start by contributing as much as you can to your retirement plan at work, whether it is a 401(k), 403(b), 457, SIMPLE IRA, or similar plan. Everyone agrees that you should not only contribute as much as you can, but you should also do your best to "max-out" your contributions, thus depositing as much as the law allows for each and every year.

This type of thinking is so pervasive that I challenge you to find a single article written in *Money* magazine, *Smart Money* magazine,

Forbes, or even *Kiplinger's* that argues against this concept. EVERYONE agrees that these plans are the best place for you to invest your money. Now, they may all argue as to what to do with your money once you get it into these plans, but they do agree that these plans are the best home for your retirement investments.

Today's retirees, however, are starting to learn that this advice, building your retirement nest egg in these traditional retirement plans, is *one of the worst decisions they have ever made!* Many of today's retirees are coming to realize that their traditional retirement plans are not designed to benefit them, but instead are designed to benefit the IRS. In fact, many are wondering whether they ended up planning for their retirement, or for the IRS's retirement.

How did we get here? How did we ever fall for the idea that traditional retirement plans were good homes for our money? Well, you might remember hearing something like this at a retirement plan meeting:

> *"Retirement plans are a great place to save for retirement. First, they offer you the opportunity to invest 'pre-tax dollars,' which means that you get a tax deduction today for the dollars you invest. Second, your money grows tax-deferred, so you don't pay tax on your money as it grows."*
>
> *"But there is a disadvantage with these plans. You will have to pay tax when you take the money out down the road. But that's OK because you will be in a lower tax bracket when you retire. Your home will be paid off and you won't need as much income, so your taxes will be less. Take the tax deduction today while you are in a higher tax bracket and pay your taxes later when you are in a lower tax bracket."*

You remember that line of thinking, don't you? What's the problem with it? The problem is that this line of thinking requires that you make several dubious assumptions. In order for this line of thinking to work out, you need to have ***all of the following be true:***

1. Taxes have to stay at the same level they are today and NOT increase down the road. (In Chapter Four, we'll learn why this is "pie-in-the-sky" thinking.)

2. Your health care expenses must not significantly increase in retirement. (Good luck there!)

3. Your lifestyle in retirement needs to be one in which you stay at home and do nothing. (Because doing something almost always costs money.)

4. And most of all, your retirement plan has to earn really lousy returns over many years. (Because no matter what the tax code is down the road, if your retirement accounts grow, you'll end up paying tax on a much larger sum as you pull the money out.)

What are the odds that *any* of the four criteria above will be met, much less all of them? Heck, you probably don't want numbers three and four to happen! I hope that you want to enjoy a comfortable retirement, where you do whatever you want to do without having to worry about money. And I sure hope that you have nice portfolio returns over time so you have a whole bunch of money to deal with during your retirement years. For most people, that's called "financial security."

This book will show you how you can build a truly comfortable retirement free of the onus of taxation. It will also show you, if you have already built large values inside of your retirement accounts, how you can potentially extract hundreds of thousands of dollars out of those accounts *without* paying tax.

One note of caution—we discuss a number of tax planning options in this book. Taxes are not simple and apply differently to everyone. We recommend that you find a qualified tax or financial advisor who can help assist you with your specific tax situation. The last chapter of this book is devoted to helping you find just such a person if you do not already have one.

The main goal of this book, however, is to help you get the IRS out of your pocket!

CHAPTER 1

A Different Perspective

"We must be willing to get rid of the life we've planned, so as to have the life that is waiting for us."
—*Joseph Campbell*

Tell me if you would take this deal: I come to you when you are thirty years old, and over the next thirty-five years, until you are sixty-five years old, I'll lend you $1,800 per year (over $60,000 total). You don't have to pay me any interest or principal over this thirty-five-year time period, not one dime.

Then for the next twenty years of your life (until you are eighty-five years old), you pay me back a total of almost $500,000. And then when you die, your children also owe me some money. They have to pay me back several hundred thousand dollars more. Would you take that deal?

What if it wasn't me lending you the money? What if it was the U.S. government? Does it really matter who lends you the money? Clearly, everyone can easily figure out that this is an absolutely crummy deal. Yet all the so-called "financial experts" recommend that you should jump at this deal! What the heck is going on here?

Whether you realize it or not, I just described a traditional IRA (or 401(k), or 403(b), or 457, etc.) where you and your spouse contribute $6,000 per year over a thirty-five-year period, starting at age thirty. With traditional retirement plans, you receive a tax benefit as you make your investment, but you then owe tax as you take your money out. *And we'll find out in just a little bit how sadly accurate the above numbers are.*

Before we go too far into these numbers, however, let's visit with Joe and Carol …

Joe and Carol

Joe and Carol are mad. They're not just mad—they are absolutely livid. They can't believe that this is happening to them! Of all people, they are the ones who deserve to enjoy a retirement carefree from worries about money. *After all, they are the ones who did exactly what all the experts told them to do.*

You see, Joe and Carol are "planners." You know the kind of people I'm talking about, they like to plan things out to the smallest detail so that everything goes smoothly. They even plan out their entire vacation's activities, day by day. So when it came to their retirement, they were no different. They meticulously planned out every detail—where they were going to live, how they were going to spend their time, and of course, where their income would come from.

Joe put together all kinds of spreadsheets over the years to make sure that their retirement savings would grow to a number large enough to support the lifestyle that they were targeting. He even figured a "low" percentage return during their retirement years so they would have some wiggle room.

They read everything they could put their hands on about retirement planning. They had subscriptions to *Kiplinger's* and *Money* magazines. They were even known to pick up the *Wall Street Journal* and *Baron's* occasionally to read up on investing. Together, they took classes on investing, and for a while, they were part of an investment club in the '90s.

If anyone would have their ducks in a row, it would be Joe and Carol. After all, they actually did what everyone said they should do. They saved 10 percent of their income and more. Joe funded his 401(k) at work, and Carol (a teacher) put money in her 403(b). They worked diligently to pay off their home so they would be able to enter retirement with no major debt other than a car payment.

They've worked hard over the years and sacrificed for their future. And now the day is here. Finally, after thirty years of work, they are able to retire into a comfortable lifestyle. So what in the world are they so worked up about?

The answer comes in one little word. It's a little word, but a powerful word. It's a word that can often mean the difference between fully enjoying retirement and just getting by. It's a word that can lay waste to years and years of planning, after doing what all the experts say you should do. It's a word that can make life seem unfair, and make you give up those "extras" that make life exciting and enjoyable. It's a little word called *taxes.*

The Bad News

Here's what happened. After their first full year of retirement, Joe was doing his taxes on TurboTax and couldn't believe the answer he was getting. He spent hours trying to figure out what he was doing wrong. Finally, in frustration, he and Carol went to visit a local Certified Public Accountant (CPA) that their friends thought highly of.

And that's what made Joe and Carol so angry. They found out that the answer that Joe was getting on TurboTax was right! They really did owe that much in tax. *It was more than they owed when they were working!* Talk about a kick in the pants.

Joe and Carol's tax return was much larger than they had ever planned on, and now they've just gone from an "easy street" retirement to a "mediocre" retirement, thanks to that one little word.

The sad news is that Joe and Carol listened to, and acted on, what "everybody" agreed was "common-sense" retirement planning. ***The problem that Joe and Carol encountered, however, was that*** *everybody's common-sense retirement planning is turning out to be just plain wrong.*

And it doesn't take a genius to figure out what happened to Joe and Carol. It is the same thing that's happening to millions of Americans throughout the country. To illustrate what's going wrong, let's consider a simple story.

Farmer Brown's Choice

Farmer Brown owns a farm that comprises hundreds of acres. Every year, his crops do well. (I know that crops don't really do well every year in the real world, but please bear with me on this.) Now, let's pretend that Farmer Brown has a choice to make. He can choose to pay tax on the small amount of seed he plants in the spring, or he can choose to pay tax on the huge crop he reaps in the fall. Which tax do you think that Farmer Brown chooses to pay every year?

Which tax would you pay, if offered the choice?

I hope you agree with me that in the fictitious example above, you, like Farmer Brown, should choose to pay tax on the seed. It's a smaller tax.

How does this relate to Joe and Carol? With their retirement plans, they saved tax on their seed, which is what all the experts say you should do. And now that they are retired, they are ending up paying tax on their harvest. This is exactly the opposite result we just agreed made sense for Farmer Brown. So why in the world would all the "experts" think this is a good idea? Let's look at another example …

John and Sara

John and Sara are married and are both thirty years old. They are starting to set aside money for retirement, and they have decided that they can afford to each invest $3,000 per year into their 401(k)s. To keep this example simple, we'll assume that they work for an employer who does not match their contributions, which is an unfortunate reality in many cases.

Figure 1-1 shows you how their money grows over the next thirty-five years, assuming an average 8 percent return and a 30 percent marginal tax bracket when combining federal and state taxes. (We'll talk more about marginal versus effective tax rates in Chapter Three.)

As you can see, over the next thirty-five years, John and Sara end up investing $210,000 and have growth of $865,257. And the part that all the CPAs like is that John and Sara get to deduct their $6,000 contribution each year, saving them $1,800 in tax every single year. Isn't that great? By taking the CPA's advice, John and Sara reduce their annual tax liability *today* by $1,800. What a great deal!

In fact, if you add it up over thirty-five years of saving, John and Sara reduce their total taxation by $63,000! This immediate benefit makes their CPA look really smart. They love their CPA. He is doing a great job helping them with their tax planning (they naively believe).

But wait, surely their investment advisor who helps them set up and manage their 401(k)s warns them about the future consequences

Figure 1-1

Age Beg. Of Year	Age End Of Year	Beginning Balance	Annual Contribution	Tax Savings	8.00% Earnings	Ending Balance
30	31	$0	$6,000	$1,800	$240	$6,240
31	32	$6,240	$6,000	$1,800	$739	$12,979
32	33	$12,979	$6,000	$1,800	$1,278	$20,258
33	34	$20,258	$6,000	$1,800	$1,861	$28,118
34	35	$28,118	$6,000	$1,800	$2,489	$36,608
35	36	$36,608	$6,000	$1,800	$3,169	$45,776
36	37	$45,776	$6,000	$1,800	$3,902	$55,678
37	38	$55,678	$6,000	$1,800	$4,694	$66,373
38	39	$66,373	$6,000	$1,800	$5,550	$77,922
39	40	$77,922	$6,000	$1,800	$6,474	$90,396
40	41	$90,396	$6,000	$1,800	$7,472	$103,868
41	42	$103,868	$6,000	$1,800	$8,549	$118,417
42	43	$118,417	$6,000	$1,800	$9,713	$134,131
43	44	$134,131	$6,000	$1,800	$10,970	$151,101
44	45	$151,101	$6,000	$1,800	$12,328	$169,429
45	46	$169,429	$6,000	$1,800	$13,794	$189,224
46	47	$189,224	$6,000	$1,800	$15,378	$210,601
47	48	$210,601	$6,000	$1,800	$17,088	$233,690
48	49	$233,690	$6,000	$1,800	$18,935	$258,625
49	50	$258,625	$6,000	$1,800	$20,930	$285,555
50	51	$285,555	$6,000	$1,800	$23,084	$314,639
51	52	$314,639	$6,000	$1,800	$25,411	$346,050
52	53	$346,050	$6,000	$1,800	$27,924	$379,974
53	54	$379,974	$6,000	$1,800	$30,638	$416,612
54	55	$416,612	$6,000	$1,800	$33,569	$456,181
55	56	$456,181	$6,000	$1,800	$36,734	$498,916
56	57	$498,916	$6,000	$1,800	$40,153	$545,069
57	58	$545,069	$6,000	$1,800	$43,846	$594,914
58	59	$594,914	$6,000	$1,800	$47,833	$648,747
59	60	$648,747	$6,000	$1,800	$52,140	$706,887
60	61	$706,887	$6,000	$1,800	$56,791	$769,678
61	62	$769,678	$6,000	$1,800	$61,814	$837,492
62	63	$837,492	$6,000	$1,800	$67,239	$910,732
63	64	$910,732	$6,000	$1,800	$73,099	$989,830
64	65	$989,830	$6,000	$1,800	$79,426	$1,075,257
		Totals:	$210,000	$63,000	$865,257	

Hypothetical only - no specific investment illustrated.

of their actions, right? Wrong! Their investment advisor follows conventional thinking (like 99 percent of other investment advisors) and actually agrees with their CPA. "401(k)s are a great vehicle for retirement monies," he assures them.

Following the advice of both their CPA and investment advisor, John and Sara fund their 401(k)s every year. Unfortunately, this is as far as their CPA's and investment advisor's advice (and all the other experts' advice) goes.

You see, after thirty-five years, John and Sara are now getting ready to retire, and they are in a bit of a tough position. Thanks to following their CPA's and investment advisor's advice over the years, they now find themselves with 100 percent of their money tied up in accounts that create taxable distributions!

Figure 1-2 shows you the severity of John and Sara's problem. We are assuming that they earn the same 8 percent rate of return, and we are also assuming that they withdraw 6 percent of their portfolio each year, as they want their annual income to increase with inflation over time. We'll also assume that at least one of them will live to age eighty-five, which is highly probable. What results do they see?

John and Sara start their retirement by withdrawing $64,515. Each year, this increases a little bit, *but how much tax are they paying on that income?* Do you remember how much tax John and Sara saved over thirty-five years' of savings? If you go back, you'll see that they saved a total of $63,000 in tax.

But what is happening now as they take money out? Every year they are paying right around $20,000 in tax. If you do the math,

Figure 1-2

Age Beg. Of Year	Age End Of Year	Beginning Balance	8.00% Earnings	6.00% Distribution	Tax Owed	Ending Balance
65	66	$1,075,257	$86,021	$64,515	$19,355	$1,096,762
66	67	$1,096,762	$87,741	$65,806	$19,742	$1,118,697
67	68	$1,118,697	$89,496	$67,122	$20,137	$1,141,071
68	69	$1,141,071	$91,286	$68,464	$20,539	$1,163,893
69	70	$1,163,893	$93,111	$69,834	$20,950	$1,187,171
70	71	$1,187,171	$94,974	$71,230	$21,369	$1,210,914
71	72	$1,210,914	$96,873	$72,655	$21,796	$1,235,132
72	73	$1,235,132	$98,811	$74,108	$22,232	$1,259,835
73	74	$1,259,835	$100,787	$75,590	$22,677	$1,285,032
74	75	$1,285,032	$102,803	$77,102	$23,131	$1,310,732
75	76	$1,310,732	$104,859	$78,644	$23,593	$1,336,947
76	77	$1,336,947	$106,956	$80,217	$24,065	$1,363,686
77	78	$1,363,686	$109,095	$81,821	$24,546	$1,390,960
78	79	$1,390,960	$111,277	$83,458	$25,037	$1,418,779
79	80	$1,418,779	$113,502	$85,127	$25,538	$1,447,154
80	81	$1,447,154	$115,772	$86,829	$26,049	$1,476,097
81	82	$1,476,097	$118,088	$88,566	$26,570	$1,505,619
82	83	$1,505,619	$120,450	$90,337	$27,101	$1,535,732
83	84	$1,535,732	$122,859	$92,144	$27,643	$1,566,446
84	85	$1,566,446	$125,316	$93,987	$28,196	$1,597,775
		Totals:	$2,090,073	$1,567,555	$470,267	

they will pay back all of the taxes they saved over thirty-five years of investing in a touch more than three short years (and that assumes that taxes don't go up down the road). And every three years after that, they will do it again, and again, and again.

In just twenty years of retirement, John and Sara will pay back over $470,000 in tax, and then they leave a $1.5 million+ account to their heirs, also taxable. What will that tax bill look like? If we use our 30 percent tax bracket (which is far too low for this amount of money), the children will owe the IRS $479,333 ($1,597,775 × 30 percent). Let's add it all up …

- John and Sara's tax bill: $470,267
- Children's tax bill: <u>$479,333</u>
- **Total tax bill:** **$949,600**

Whose retirement were John and Sara planning for—their's or the IRS's? John and Sara, following the advice of their CPA and investment advisor, were able to save $63,000 over thirty-five years of investing. But this advice led them to a destination where they and their children had to pay the IRS back over $900,000 during the last twenty years of their lives.

The CPA and investment advisor are now telling John and Sara that they shouldn't complain about their taxes now, because it means that they have money. What do you think? Would John and Sara have taken that $1,800 tax savings each year if they knew where that would lead them?

John and Sara would have been far better off to have paid their tax on their seed (their investment) and enjoyed a tax-free harvest down the road. Traditional retirement planning may save you tax today, *but it completely fails you in retirement as you pay those savings back over and over and over again.*

Summary

At the beginning of this chapter, we talked about what a rotten deal traditional retirement plans turn out to be. Then we learned how Joe and Carol were so upset after years of doing everything they thought was good and solid planning. Are you starting to get a glimpse of what they could have done differently?

We also looked at John and Sara. Like Joe and Carol, they followed the advice of their CPA and investment advisor, which fell along the lines of conventional thinking. The results of this traditional thinking turned out to be pretty ugly for John and Sara (although the IRS had nothing to complain about).

This book was written to both help younger people like John and Sara do a better job of planning for their retirement, and to help people like Joe and Carol get out of the mess they are in.

If you are younger and just starting out like John and Sara, this book has the potential to help you build a retirement full of tax-free income. Tax-free income in retirement can help you truly enjoy your "Golden Years."

If you find yourself in the position of Joe and Carol, then this book will show you how to get out of the mess you are in. But traditional thinking will not do the trick. It's time for you to start thinking a little bit differently than the rest of the crowd.

Remember, if "everyone" was right, we'd all be rich and happy. Since we aren't all rich and happy, maybe "everyone" has a few things to learn.

CHAPTER 2

A Qualified Retirement Plan Primer

"We are continually faced by great opportunities brilliantly disguised as insoluble problems."

—Lee Iacocca

Before we go too far, we should take a moment to review some history and how we got to where we are today. While you don't need to know all of the intricate details of qualified retirement plan law, having a working knowledge of the broad brushstrokes of the history of qualified plans should be helpful.

The passing of the Employee Retirement Income Security Act (ERISA) in 1974 kicked off the modern age of qualified retirement plans. Included in ERISA was the birth of the Individual Retirement Account (IRA). Four years later, the Revenue Act of 1978 included a provision that became widely known as Internal Revenue Code (IRC) 401(k), and the retirement planning dam broke open. By the early 1980s, the IRS was issuing regulations clarifying the new 401(k) rules, corporations were adopting 401(k) plans left and right, and the rush was on!

Why were these plans so popular? And why do they continue to be so popular today? It all comes down to taxes.

Benefits of Qualified Retirement Plans

Qualified Retirement Plans, which now include 401(k), 403(b), 457, IRA, SIMPLE IRA, SEP IRA, and Profit Sharing (just to name a few), all offer some interesting tax benefits. And it's because of these benefits that CPAs, investment professionals, and the financial press recommend them so highly.

Pre-Tax Dollars

First, as you deposit money into these accounts, you get to deduct your deposit off of your income for tax purposes. This is often called "pre-tax dollars," and it simply means that the money goes into the plan before it is taxed. How does this benefit you?

Well, let's assume that you are married, and between you and your spouse, you have a household income of $80,000. You both contribute $5,000 to your company 401(k)s for a total of $10,000 each year. Thanks to the "pre-tax dollar" feature, instead of being taxed on $80,000 of income, you are only taxed on $70,000 of income. If your marginal tax rate was 30 percent (federal and state), you would save $3,000 on your income tax for the year. As you can imagine, CPAs start drooling when they get to tell you that they saved you $3,000 in tax for the past year!

This is a really easy way for your CPA to show you how hard he/she is working for you, and the benefit they bring to you. It's too bad that they don't also tell you how the $3,000 you are saving today will explode into many extra thousands of dollars in taxes down the road.

Tax-Deferral

In addition to being able to invest pre-tax dollars, Qualified Retirement Plans also allow your money to grow in a tax-deferred environment. In other words, you don't pay tax on your growth until you take your money out down the road. This can be a significant benefit! Do you remember John and Sara from our last chapter? They were thirty years old and planning on contributing $6,000 per year to their retirement plans over the next thirty years. You might recall that by the time they reach age sixty-five, their plan values would be worth more than $1 million.

Let's find out what their retirement plans would be worth if they had to pay tax on their gains each year. Now, we need to be aware that John and Sara would have two different tax rates that may apply to their investments. First, they have ordinary income rates, which we'll assume to be the same 30 percent figure we've been using so far. Second, they have capital gains rates, which are 15 percent for almost everyone.

We need to make one more assumption. We need to determine what amount of their gains would be taxed at which rate. For the purposes of this analysis, we'll assume the following:

- 2/3 of gains at capital gains rates: $2/3 \times 15\% = 10\%$
- 1/3 of gains at ordinary income rates: $\underline{1/3 \times 30\% = 10\%}$
- Total blended tax rate: $10\% + 10\% = \mathbf{20\%}$

We cannot forget that in this example, John and Sara would be investing after-tax dollars. That means that instead of having $6,000 to invest each year, they only have $4,200 ($6,000 less 30 percent tax) to invest. Figure 2-1 shows you how this approach turns out for John and Sara, assuming that they earn the same 8 percent return that we've been using.

Wow, what a difference in values. Here, John and Sara have a bit less than half of the account value as before, all because of the combination of pre-tax dollars and tax-deferral!

Figure 2-2 compares the two accounts and the income that they generate for John and Sara.

Which would you rather have—$45,161 to spend or $30,868? This is a difference of $14,292 per year. If you live twenty years in retirement, we are talking about a difference in income of over $280,000! Could you figure out a way to spend that extra $280,000? Are you starting to see the benefit of tax deferral?

Figure 2-1

Age Beg. Of Year	Age End Of Year	Beginning Balance	Annual Contribution	8.00% Earnings	Less Taxes	Ending Balance
30	31	$0	$4,200	$168	$34	$4,334
31	32	$4,334	$4,200	$515	$103	$8,946
32	33	$8,946	$4,200	$884	$177	$13,853
33	34	$13,853	$4,200	$1,276	$255	$19,074
34	35	$19,074	$4,200	$1,694	$339	$24,629
35	36	$24,629	$4,200	$2,138	$428	$30,540
36	37	$30,540	$4,200	$2,611	$522	$36,829
37	38	$36,829	$4,200	$3,114	$623	$43,520
38	39	$43,520	$4,200	$3,650	$730	$50,640
39	40	$50,640	$4,200	$4,219	$844	$58,215
40	41	$58,215	$4,200	$4,825	$965	$66,276
41	42	$66,276	$4,200	$5,470	$1,094	$74,852
42	43	$74,852	$4,200	$6,156	$1,231	$83,977
43	44	$83,977	$4,200	$6,886	$1,377	$93,686
44	45	$93,686	$4,200	$7,663	$1,533	$104,016
45	46	$104,016	$4,200	$8,489	$1,698	$115,007
46	47	$115,007	$4,200	$9,369	$1,874	$126,702
47	48	$126,702	$4,200	$10,304	$2,061	$139,145
48	49	$139,145	$4,200	$11,300	$2,260	$152,385
49	50	$152,385	$4,200	$12,359	$2,472	$166,472
50	51	$166,472	$4,200	$13,486	$2,697	$181,461
51	52	$181,461	$4,200	$14,685	$2,937	$197,409
52	53	$197,409	$4,200	$15,961	$3,192	$214,377
53	54	$214,377	$4,200	$17,318	$3,464	$232,432
54	55	$232,432	$4,200	$18,763	$3,753	$251,642
55	56	$251,642	$4,200	$20,299	$4,060	$272,081
56	57	$272,081	$4,200	$21,934	$4,387	$293,829
57	58	$293,829	$4,200	$23,674	$4,735	$316,968
58	59	$316,968	$4,200	$25,525	$5,105	$341,589
59	60	$341,589	$4,200	$27,495	$5,499	$367,785
60	61	$367,785	$4,200	$29,591	$5,918	$395,657
61	62	$395,657	$4,200	$31,821	$6,364	$425,314
62	63	$425,314	$4,200	$34,193	$6,839	$456,868
63	64	$456,868	$4,200	$36,717	$7,343	$490,442
64	65	$490,442	$4,200	$39,403	$7,881	$526,165
		Totals:	$147,000	$473,956	$94,791	

Hypothetical only - no specific investment illustrated.

Figure 2-2

Qualified Plan	
Account Balance:	$1,075,257
6% Income:	$64,515
Less Tax*:	$19,355
Net Income:	$45,161

Non-Qualified Plan	
Account Balance:	$526,165
6% Income:	$42,093
Less Tax*:	$11,225
Net Income:	$30,868

Annual Difference:	$14,292

*Note: only income from the qualified plan is taxed as it is taken out, not the earnings. 100% of the earnings from the non-qualified plan are taxed, not just the income.

Hypothetical only - no specific invesetment illustrated.

This comparison is the foundation of why all the so-called "experts" recommend traditional retirement plans. This is the core of their line of reasoning. We've already put a pretty big dent in this thinking in our last chapter looking at John and Sara, and in future chapters, we'll finish the job as we discuss new and creative tax-free retirement planning strategies.

The Company Match

The last major benefit of Qualified Retirement Plans is that some of them, particularly 401(k) plans, offer a company match. In other words, if you put a certain percentage of your income in, then the company you work for matches your contributions up to a certain amount.

For example, a common matching program works like this: Your company might match your contributions fifty cents for each dollar you put in, up to a maximum of 6 percent of your contributions. Let's look at how this works.

Assume that you earn $50,000 per year and you contribute 10 percent of your income. The total amount contributed to your retirement account for the year looks like this:

- Your contribution: $50,000 × 10% = $5,000
- Company match: $50,000 × 6% × 50% = $1,500
- Total contribution: $6,500

The $1,500 that your company kicked in represents "free" money. It represents an immediate return on your investment. If your company matches your contributions, you need to put in at least enough each year to get the full match. Otherwise, you are throwing away money.

If your company matches your contributions with any reasonable amount, then you are in one of the very few positions where putting money into a traditional retirement plan is a good idea. And then, you should only invest enough to get the company match, *and not a dollar more.*

Other Benefits

Finally, some argue that a benefit of Qualified Retirement Plans is the automatic deduction feature with many of these plans. Many of these plans provide you the option of having your company deduct your contribution from your paycheck automatically. That way, the money is deposited into your retirement account before you get it.

These people argue that if the money wasn't automatically deducted from their paycheck, then you might spend the money versus saving it. In other words, they argue that you would not have the financial discipline to save for your future.

The unfortunate reality is that in many cases, they are right. Far too many people do not have the discipline to save versus spend everything they earn.

But I don't include this as a benefit for you reading this. You are clearly a person who is financially disciplined, or you wouldn't be reading this book right now.

The Strings Attached

You know that when the government giveth, the government taketh away! In Qualified Retirement Plans, the government giveth in the form of the tax benefits discussed above. The government taketh away through the strings they attach to these types of plans.

Limits on Your Contributions

The first string comes in the form of a limitation on how much money you can invest in any one year. The government says that you can only take advantage of these plans to a certain degree. You can find the most current limitations in *IRS Publication 590* (www.irs.gov). In addition, we have included the most recent limitations as of this writing in Appendix A. For your reference, *Publication 590* is the IRS's primary resource on IRAs and other Qualified Retirement Plans.

Limits on Access to Your Own Money

The second string has to do with liquidity. These plans are intended for retirement, and the government has dictated that this money, for the most part, should not be accessed prior to age 59½. (Please don't ask me where 59½ comes from—I can't find anyone who can explain the logic of the government.) The government has determined that "normal" retirement age occurs after 59½, so that's when you can access this money without penalty. If you try to take money out of your Qualified Retirement Plans prior to age 59½, then you not only pay income tax on your distribution, you also pay a 10 percent penalty tax.

Fortunately, the government is not completely heartless, and they have certain exceptions to the 10 percent penalty. You can take money out of your Qualified Retirement Plans without the 10 percent penalty for the following reasons:

- Death
- Permanent or total disability
- Series of substantial and equal periodic payments (referenced by I.R.C. 72(t), which is a bit complex and outside the scope of this book)
- Medical expenses exceeding 7.5 percent of your adjusted gross income
- Medical insurance premiums after losing your job
- College expenses for yourself or a dependent
- Home purchase (maximum of $10,000 and additional conditions apply)

It is important that you know that some of the above exceptions apply to IRAs only. This is another area where you really need to sit down with your financial or tax advisor to obtain appropriate clarification for your circumstances. You should also consult *IRS Publication 590*.

Limits on How Long You Can Invest

The third string has to do with forced distributions. Whether you want to or not, when you reach the age of 70½ you must begin to take a certain amount out of your Qualified Retirement Plan each year. It's called your Required Minimum Distribution (RMD). We'll talk about RMD calculations in detail in the next chapter.

The mindset of the government here is that this money is for your retirement—NOT just a haven to grow your money tax-deferred to give to your children someday. So how does the IRS force this distribution on you? Simple—if you do not take out an amount of money at least equal to your RMD, then the IRS hits you with a 50 percent penalty on the shortfall.

In other words, the IRS thinks that it is **five times worse** to keep your money in these plans too long than to take the money out early. Why do they take this approach? Again, simple. The IRS doesn't collect tax until you pull money out of your account. It is not in the best interests of the IRS or the government for you to keep your money in there forever. They want to collect.

Like pretty much every other tax law, this one also has a couple of exceptions. The primary exception has to do with if you are still working past age 70½. In that case, you may have the ability to postpone your RMDs. This is an area that you should closely discuss with your CPA or financial advisor to ensure you don't make a mistake, given the size of the penalties.

Limits on Investment Options

A fourth string limits the investments that you can have inside of your Qualified Retirement Plan. This is most commonly seen in the non-IRA plans. For example, a typical 401(k) has a menu of twenty to fifty mutual funds to select from. You choose one or several of those funds to invest in, and you cannot go outside of those choices.

It's like going to a restaurant where you are offered no exceptions to the menu. You must eat from the menu in front of you, with no alterations. If you want filet mignon and it's not on the menu, then too bad. You need to pick something else for dinner.

IRAs, on the other hand, allow for a much wider range of investment options, with the exception of collectibles, large amounts of precious metals, and other alternative investments. Other than that, the IRA "restaurant" has just about anything on the menu, and alterations are usually acceptable.

Summary

Qualified Retirement Plans have a number of benefits that provide you instant and ongoing gratification. Primary among them are the tax-deduction of your contribution and the tax-deferred growth. Of course, you have strings attached in order to receive these benefits, but for most people, they are not restraining enough to tie them down.

Qualified Retirement Plans are lauded throughout the financial press and investment community, mostly due to the tax benefits described. But as you are already starting to learn, they also have an ugly side that you find out about when it's very late in the game. And in the next chapter, we're going to discuss that ugly side in detail. For many people, it makes the benefits seem paltry by comparison.

CHAPTER 3

Consequences of QRPs

*"Sooner or later everyone sits down to a banquet of
consequences."*

—Robert Louis Stevenson

In the last chapter, we reviewed a number of the benefits provided by Qualified Retirement Plans. Now we need to discover whether the benefits you gain are greater than the eventual costs you pay.

Before we have that discussion, you first need to have a decent understanding of the difference between marginal and effective tax rates (something very few people understand). So let's jump right in.

Marginal versus Effective Tax Rates

"Effective" tax rates are defined as your total tax owed divided by your total income. In other words, this is that tax rate that you pay on *all* of your income. Let's look at a simple example for federal tax rates, and ignoring state taxes.

Assume that your total income from all sources is $75,000. Let's also assume that your total tax liability is $7,500. Your *effective tax rate* is calculated like this:

- Total income: $75,000
- Divided by total tax: $7,500
- Equals "effective" tax rate: **10%**

"Marginal" tax rates, on the other hand, represent the tax rate that you would pay *on the next dollar earned.* In other words, if you received a raise of $5,000 (so your new household income is now $80,000 total) *to what degree would you pay tax on that extra $5,000?* Is it 10 percent, or something else?

In America, we have a "graduated" tax system. This means that the more you earn, the higher tax rate you pay. In our example, if you are married, then an increase from $75,000 of household income to $80,000 would be taxed at a *marginal tax rate* of 25 percent for federal taxes (based on the tax code as of this writing). So what would that number be?

- $5,000 × 25% =   **$1,250**

Compare this with the result you would expect if you were using your *effective* tax bracket of 10 percent.

- $5,000 × 10% =   **$500**

This is a big difference! Your $5,000 raise cost you $1,250 in tax, not the $500 you might have been expecting.

So far, we have been ignoring any state taxes that would be piled on top of the federal tax. If you live in a high income tax state, such as California or New York, then this can be a significant addition, even for low-income people. Other states, like Texas and Florida, have no income tax. Overall, the average state income tax is pretty close to 5 percent throughout the country.

Most people in America find themselves in the 25 percent marginal tax bracket. When you combine the average state tax of 5 percent, then we learn that most people have a combined marginal tax bracket of 30 percent.

For simplicity, throughout the rest of this book, all calculations will use a marginal tax bracket of 30 percent. Clearly, your individual marginal tax bracket may be different, and you need to take that into account for your individual planning.

The Impact of Marginal Tax Rates

You're probably wondering why I'm spending so much time talking about the difference between effective and marginal rates. The reason is that when it comes to your financial planning, marginal tax rates are far more important that effective tax rates.

Why is that the case? Well, I gave you a clue in the previous section. If you get an increase in your income, which tax rate applied—effective or marginal? Marginal did. What if your income goes down, which tax rate will apply? You're right—marginal.

What do CPAs do when they focus on tax planning? They are doing their best to intentionally reduce your taxable income. Every new tax deduction that they can discover reduces your taxable income by some degree. Then they calculate the value of their planning based on marginal tax rates.

This book focuses on Qualified Retirement Plans. When you take money out of them, it is considered an addition to your other income. Therefore, the distribution is taxed at your marginal rate.

As you can see, when it comes to your financial planning, your marginal tax rate is a vital statistic for you to know!

Consequences of Qualified Retirement Plans (QRPs)

Back in Chapter One, we provided you an illustration of John and Sara. You may recall that they were thirty years old and were beginning to save $6,000 per year in their QRPs. We learned that over thirty-five years of investing, they ended up with the following results:

- Total tax savings on investment: **$63,000**

- Total taxes owed on retirement income: $470,267
- Total taxes owed by children: $479,333
- Total taxes owed from investment: **$949,600**

Because John and Sara followed the advice of their CPA and investment advisor, they eventually ended up paying back their tax savings at a rate of approximately $15 to $1. In other words, for every dollar that they saved in taxation during their accumulation years, they ended up paying back $15.

From the viewpoint of the IRS, this sounds like a pretty good deal. What kind of deal does it look like from John and Sara's perspective?

Required Minimum Distributions

Now, some of you reading this may be thinking that I am stacking the deck here. You may be saying to yourself, "Those numbers are true, but who takes income out of their QRPs each year anyway? Don't most people just leave the money in there and only take out the small percentage each year that they are forced to when they turn age 70½? I'm sure that those people do much better with their tax planning."

You know what? Many people do exactly that. They only take out the minimum that they are forced to withdraw. Before we go into the numbers in this type of situation, let's take a moment and think about what these people are doing.

These folks work hard and sacrifice to build a nice little nest egg for their retirement. They accumulate a decent amount of money in their QRPs. And then, they choose not to take any money out. They choose to leave their money in their retirement plan to continue to grow tax-deferred. They only take money out when the government forces them to, and even then, they only take out the minimum that they have to.

Personally, I have to tell you that I find this a little bit sad. It's just like working for thirty-five years to build a wonderful home, only to leave it sit empty once it's completed. And you only use it after you turn 70½ years old because the government forces you to. Even then, you only use this beautiful home for the minimum amount of time each year that the government forces you to. Other than that, it sits empty.

Isn't that a ridiculous concept? You can't take your money with you when you leave this earth. Why not use it to generate additional income for you to use to make your Golden Years truly Golden?

That being said, let's go back to our question: Would these folks do better with their tax planning if all they took out was their required minimum distributions? After all, they are not taking out as much money (and paying tax on it), right?

Calculating Required Minimum Distributions

The first step is to make sure that everyone knows what we're talking about. You may recall in Chapter Two, I referenced something called a Required Minimum Distribution. One of the strings attached to QRPs is that when you reach a certain age (70½), you must begin taking money out of your retirement plan each year. But how do you determine how much you must take?

The good news is that it's really pretty simple. The IRS has a table called the Uniform Distribution Table that you can find in *Publication 590* (www.irs.gov). We've included a copy in the back of this book in Appendix B. This table applies to everyone with the exception of people who have a spouse that is more than ten years younger than they are.

In this table, you look up what your age will be at the end of the year and find the "divisor" that applies to that age. Then, you take your total QRP balances as of December 31 of last year, and divide into that number the divisor you found in the Uniform Distribution Table.

For example, let's say that by the end of this year you will be seventy-five years old. You look up your divisor on the Uniform Distribution Table and find it to be 22.9.

Then, you find your total QRP values as of December 31 of last year. Let's say that your QRP balances totaled $229,000. So what is your required distribution for this year?

- $229,000/22.9 =   **$10,000**

That's all there is to it! Each year, you look up your new divisor.

During the year, the IRS doesn't care when you withdraw the money. You could take it out month-by-month, quarter-by-quarter, or just whenever you feel like it. All the IRS wants you to do is get your minimum distribution out by the end of the year. They don't even care which account you pull the money out of—just get it out.

Can you withdraw more than the minimum? Sure—but remember, you are calculating your *minimum* distribution, not your maximum. But if you don't pull out enough, you should remember from the last chapter that the IRS will hit you with a 50 percent penalty on top of your normal income tax, so don't pull out too little!

So, how would just taking out just the required minimum distribution each year work out for John and Sara? We learned a little bit earlier that their QRPs worked out really well *for the IRS* when they withdrew income each year to live on. Would it work out better for John and Sara if they only took out (and paid tax on) their minimum amount? Figure 3-1 shows you the results of this approach.

As you can see, the good news under this plan is that John and Sara only pay slightly less than $460,000 in tax compared to paying a bit more than $470,000 when they took income right away. They saved $10,000! Unfortunately, $10,000 isn't nearly enough to make

Figure 3-1

Age Beg. Of Year	Age End Of Year	Beginning Balance	8.00% Earnings	RMD Divisor	Required Distribution	Less Tax @ 30%	Ending Balance
65	66	$1,075,257	$86,021		$0	$0	$1,161,278
66	67	$1,161,278	$92,902		$0	$0	$1,254,180
67	68	$1,254,180	$100,334		$0	$0	$1,354,514
68	69	$1,354,514	$108,361		$0	$0	$1,462,875
69	70	$1,462,875	$117,030		$0	$0	$1,579,905
70	71	$1,579,905	$126,392	27.4	$57,661	$17,298	$1,648,637
71	72	$1,648,637	$131,891	26.5	$62,213	$18,664	$1,718,315
72	73	$1,718,315	$137,465	25.6	$67,122	$20,137	$1,788,659
73	74	$1,788,659	$143,093	24.7	$72,415	$21,725	$1,859,336
74	75	$1,859,336	$148,747	23.8	$78,123	$23,437	$1,929,960
75	76	$1,929,960	$154,397	22.9	$84,278	$25,283	$2,000,079
76	77	$2,000,079	$160,006	22	$90,913	$27,274	$2,069,172
77	78	$2,069,172	$165,534	21.2	$97,602	$29,281	$2,137,104
78	79	$2,137,104	$170,968	20.3	$105,276	$31,583	$2,202,796
79	80	$2,202,796	$176,224	19.5	$112,964	$33,889	$2,266,056
80	81	$2,266,056	$181,284	18.7	$121,179	$36,354	$2,326,161
81	82	$2,326,161	$186,093	17.9	$129,953	$38,986	$2,382,300
82	83	$2,382,300	$190,584	17.1	$139,316	$41,795	$2,433,569
83	84	$2,433,569	$194,685	16.3	$149,299	$44,790	$2,478,955
84	85	$2,478,955	$198,316	15.5	$159,933	$47,980	$2,517,339
					Totals: $1,528,246	$458,474	

Hypothetical only - no specific investment illustrated.

much of a difference here. Both numbers are a whole lot more than the $63,000 they saved over the last thirty-five years.

The bad news is that in both cases, John and Sara aren't done with their taxes yet. Remember, they have money left over in their QRP at death. This money goes to their children (or any other beneficiary), but it's NOT tax-free. Before, we calculated that the children would owe $479,333 in tax. What would the tax bill be to the children in this example (not including any inheritance taxes)?

- $2,517,339 × 30% =   **$755,202**

Again, we need to be aware that using a 30 percent rate for an account of this size is pretty unrealistic. It would almost certainly be higher.

In this scenario, the total taxation of John and Sara's QRPs now adds up to the following:

- John and Sara's tax bill: $458,474
- Children's tax bill: $755,202
- Total tax bill: **$1,213,676**

That's a lot of money to pay back to the IRS, just so John and Sara could save $63,000!

The bottom line is that it just doesn't matter whether John and Sara take income right away from their retirement plans, or if they wait and take out only the required minimum. Either way, the IRS enjoys a huge amount of tax revenues at John and Sara's expense. *And that's assuming that taxes don't increase down the road.*

What happened here? When it comes down to it, John and Sara saved tax on their "seed" only to pay tax later on their much larger "harvest." For John and Sara, this decision led to a devastating result. Just imagine all the things they could have done during their retirement years if they had all that tax money to spend on themselves and their family, instead of sending it away to the IRS.

The "Stretch" IRA

One of the most popular concepts discussed today is the "Stretch" IRA. What is a Stretch IRA? A Stretch IRA is a phrase that describes the manner in which a beneficiary takes a stream of payments from an inherited IRA, instead of cashing in the whole account at one time. Starting in 2007, the Pension Protection Act allows pretty much any beneficiary of a QRP to take their inheritance in the form of a Stretch IRA if they choose.

This means that after John and Sara die, their children don't have to cash in the QRPs and pay all that tax upfront. Instead, with the Stretch IRA option, the IRS allows them to calculate their own minimum distribution and withdraw just that small amount. The "common-sense" thinking is that this way, the beneficiaries get to continue the tax-deferral over their lifetimes. And because they are taking less money out each year, their tax burden should be lessened, or at least better managed.

By this point, you should be questioning in your mind if this is really the best deal for them. After all, tax deferral certainly didn't help John and Sara! Why should continuing tax deferral help their children?

Let's run some numbers to find out if this Stretch concept makes sense. We will have to make a couple of assumptions. We'll assume that John and Sara have two children, Mark and Susan. Mark is the oldest and he is thirty years younger than John and Sara. Susan is two years younger than Mark.

We'll keep the investment returns the same, and to make this a bit simpler, we'll assume that John and Sara die at the same time, when they are eighty-five years of age. That will make Mark fifty-five and Susan fifty-three. Our final assumption will be that John and Sara took income right away when they retired, so they will leave a total of $1,597,775 (which we'll round off to $1.6 million) to Mark and Susan.

Here's how this works. Mark and Susan will each look up their age on the Single Life Expectancy Table for Inherited IRAs, which is also found in *IRS Publication 590* (www.irs.gov). You can also find this table in the back of this book in Appendix C. Mark looks up his age, fifty-five, and learns that his initial divisor is 29.6. Susan's is 31.4.

Each of them divides their share of the QRP by their divisor. Each year after that, they subtract 1 from their previous year's divisor to calculate the new minimum distribution. Figure 3-2 shows you Mark's Stretch IRA and Figure 3-3 shows you Susan's.

Figure 3-2

Age	Beginning Balance	8.00% Earnings	Divisor	Amount Distributed	Ending Balance
55	$800,000	$64,000	29.6	$27,027	**$836,973**
56	$836,973	$66,958	28.6	$29,265	**$874,666**
57	$874,666	$69,973	27.6	$31,691	**$912,949**
58	$912,949	$73,036	26.6	$34,321	**$951,663**
59	$951,663	$76,133	25.6	$37,174	**$990,622**
60	$990,622	$79,250	24.6	$40,269	**$1,029,602**
61	$1,029,602	$82,368	23.6	$43,627	**$1,068,343**
62	$1,068,343	$85,467	22.6	$47,272	**$1,106,539**
63	$1,106,539	$88,523	21.6	$51,229	**$1,143,833**
64	$1,143,833	$91,507	20.6	$55,526	**$1,179,814**
65	$1,179,814	$94,385	19.6	$60,195	**$1,214,005**
66	$1,214,005	$97,120	18.6	$65,269	**$1,245,856**
67	$1,245,856	$99,668	17.6	$70,787	**$1,274,737**
68	$1,274,737	$101,979	16.6	$76,791	**$1,299,925**
69	$1,299,925	$103,994	15.6	$83,329	**$1,320,590**
70	$1,320,590	$105,647	14.6	$90,451	**$1,335,786**
71	$1,335,786	$106,863	13.6	$98,220	**$1,344,429**
72	$1,344,429	$107,554	12.6	$106,701	**$1,345,283**
73	$1,345,283	$107,623	11.6	$115,973	**$1,336,933**
74	$1,336,933	$106,955	10.6	$126,126	**$1,317,762**
75	$1,317,762	$105,421	9.6	$137,267	**$1,285,916**
76	$1,285,916	$102,873	8.6	$149,525	**$1,239,264**
77	$1,239,264	$99,141	7.6	$163,061	**$1,175,344**
78	$1,175,344	$94,028	6.6	$178,082	**$1,091,289**
79	$1,091,289	$87,303	5.6	$194,873	**$983,719**
80	$983,719	$78,698	4.6	$213,852	**$848,565**
81	$848,565	$67,885	3.6	$235,712	**$680,738**
82	$680,738	$54,459	2.6	$261,822	**$473,374**
83	$473,374	$37,870	1.6	$295,859	**$215,385**
84	$215,385	$17,231	1	$232,616	**$0**

Total Taxable Distributions: $3,353,912

Hypothetical only - no specific investment illustrated.

Figure 3-3

Age	Beginning Balance	8.00% Earnings	Divisor	Amount Distributed	Ending Balance
53	$800,000	$64,000	31.4	$25,478	**$838,522**
54	$838,522	$67,082	30.4	$27,583	**$878,021**
55	$878,021	$70,242	29.4	$29,865	**$918,398**
56	$918,398	$73,472	28.4	$32,338	**$959,532**
57	$959,532	$76,763	27.4	$35,019	**$1,001,275**
58	$1,001,275	$80,102	26.4	$37,927	**$1,043,450**
59	$1,043,450	$83,476	25.4	$41,081	**$1,085,845**
60	$1,085,845	$86,868	24.4	$44,502	**$1,128,211**
61	$1,128,211	$90,257	23.4	$48,214	**$1,170,254**
62	$1,170,254	$93,620	22.4	$52,243	**$1,211,631**
63	$1,211,631	$96,930	21.4	$56,618	**$1,251,943**
64	$1,251,943	$100,155	20.4	$61,370	**$1,290,729**
65	$1,290,729	$103,258	19.4	$66,532	**$1,327,454**
66	$1,327,454	$106,196	18.4	$72,144	**$1,361,507**
67	$1,361,507	$108,921	17.4	$78,248	**$1,392,180**
68	$1,392,180	$111,374	16.4	$84,889	**$1,418,665**
69	$1,418,665	$113,493	15.4	$92,121	**$1,440,037**
70	$1,440,037	$115,203	14.4	$100,003	**$1,455,237**
71	$1,455,237	$116,419	13.4	$108,600	**$1,463,057**
72	$1,463,057	$117,045	12.4	$117,988	**$1,462,113**
73	$1,462,113	$116,969	11.4	$128,256	**$1,450,826**
74	$1,450,826	$116,066	10.4	$139,503	**$1,427,390**
75	$1,427,390	$114,191	9.4	$151,850	**$1,389,731**
76	$1,389,731	$111,178	8.4	$165,444	**$1,335,465**
77	$1,335,465	$106,837	7.4	$180,468	**$1,261,834**
78	$1,261,834	$100,947	6.4	$197,162	**$1,165,619**
79	$1,165,619	$93,250	5.4	$215,855	**$1,043,014**
80	$1,043,014	$83,441	4.4	$237,049	**$889,406**
81	$889,406	$71,152	3.4	$261,590	**$698,969**
82	$698,969	$55,917	2.4	$291,237	**$463,649**
83	$463,649	$37,092	1.4	$331,178	**$169,563**
84	$169,563	$13,565	1	$183,128	**$0**

Total Taxable Distributions: $3,695,482

Hypothetical only - no specific investment illustrated.

Adding It All Up

The good news for Mark and Susan is that they are able to turn an inheritance worth $1.6 million into a lifelong distribution stream of over $7 million between them. The bad news is that *it's all taxable!* Let's calculate this tax bill.

- Mark: $3,353,912 × 30% = $1,006,174
- Susan: $3,695,482 × 30% = $1,108,645
- Total Stretch tax bill: **$2,114,819**

We don't want to forget that during their lifetimes, John and Sara also paid $470,267 of tax on their distributions …

- John and Sara's tax bill: $470,267
- Children's Stretch tax bill: $2,114,819
- **Total tax bill:**   **$2,585,086**

What do you think about that consequence? A $2.5 million tax bill payable to the IRS just so John and Sara can save $63,000 during thirty-five years of accumulation. Given the choice, what would you do?: Would you choose to pay the $63,000 up front and have the $2.5 million to spend tax-free in retirement, or would you save the $63,000 and owe the $2.5 million tax later? It's a pretty easy decision, isn't it?

Please don't misunderstand me. I believe that anyone would have a hard time complaining if they were in Mark and Susan's position. My point is simply this—the IRS collected handsomely against John and Sara, and now it just keeps collecting from their children. This is outrageous!

Summary

In this chapter, we discussed the tax consequences to John and Sara as they take distributions in retirement. We learned that no matter how they did it, they ended up paying the IRS several times the amount of money they saved while accumulating their accounts.

We then evaluated the different methods that their children might use to receive their inheritance. Again, they ended up paying the IRS hundreds of thousands, if not millions, of dollars in taxes depending on the method they used.

The sad news is that all of this happened just so John and Sara could receive a tax deduction up front. They saved taxes on their "seed" of $63,000 and ended up paying those savings back over, and over, and over again. When all was said and done, traditional retirement planning worked out very well for the IRS to the detriment of John, Sara and their children.

John and Sara saved $63,000. The IRS collected back hundreds of thousands of dollars in return. What a crummy deal for John and Sara!

The problem that traditional retirement planning has is that it all focuses on the total dollar amounts, *but it ignores the tax impact* of those dollars. By ignoring the tax impact, you end up in a much different position than you may ever expect.

CHAPTER 4

The Future of Taxation

"… in this world nothing is certain but death and taxes."
—*Benjamin Franklin*

I'm sure that at some point in your life, you've heard the so-called "financial experts" tell you the following:

"When it comes to your retirement planning, take your tax break today while you are earning a higher amount of income. After all, when you are retired, your income will be lower, so your tax bracket will be lower. So take your tax break today at the higher rate and pay taxes later at a lower rate."

You've heard that, haven't you? It's standard advice given at every single 401(k) or 403(b) meeting every day throughout the country.

Hopefully, you already have figured out why this is such awful advice. From the last chapter, we saw John and Sara take this advice and save $63,000 over thirty-five years. However, in the end, they ended up paying back over $450,000, and their children paid even more.

When all is said and done, there are two more major problems with this line of thinking:

Major Problem Number One: Your Income Will Be Lower in Retirement So Your Tax Rate Will Be Lower

Let's address this one by asking you a very simple question. Imagine yourself sacrificing and saving for twenty, thirty, or even forty years for retirement. After years and years of setting money aside, the time has come for you to retire. *At what standard of living do you wish to retire?* If you are like 99 percent of people, you would like either the same standard of living as before retirement, or even a little higher, because you may wish to travel.

Here's another simple question: *If you want to enjoy the same standard of living as you did right before you retired, how much income will you need in retirement?* The answer is pretty simple, isn't it? You need pretty much the same amount of income (less retirement contributions) as before.

Next question: *If you will need about the same amount of income after retirement as you had before, exactly how will your income taxes go down?*

I know what many of you are thinking. "Wait one minute here, buster! I won't need as much income in retirement, because my house will be paid for free and clear. I won't have that big mortgage payment to make, so I can get along with less income."

This is a very nice thought. And it may be true—you may have your home paid for, so you may not have a mortgage payment. But what kind of payment might you have in retirement that will likely be as large, if not larger, than your mortgage payment?

The Reality of Healthcare

Think about what happens to your body as you age. It starts breaking down, doesn't it? And what happens when your body starts breaking down? Obviously, the doctor visits become much more frequent and expensive. The bottom line is that your home may be paid for, but your healthcare expenses are now as large, or larger, than your mortgage ever was. You ignore this very real expense in retirement at your peril!

"But wait a minute," you may be thinking. "When I retire, my company will pay for my health insurance, it's one of my retirement benefits." Perhaps it is, but will your company be able to continue those benefits throughout your retirement? Why not ask some General Motors or Ford retirees how that plan is working for them?

Your Retirement Lifestyle

Finally, think about what you want your retirement to be. What will you be doing? Will you be traveling? Visiting grandchildren? Golfing or playing tennis? Going on a cruise every now and then? What do all these activities have in common? You're right, ***they all cost money***!

Unless you plan on being a couch potato, almost everything you do in retirement costs money. Often, people want to do all the things in retirement that they did not have the time to do during their working careers. Almost every one of those things cost money.

And don't forget, if you have children, what's going on in their lives? They probably live somewhere else in the country. They are busy with their careers and are starting, or in the middle of, having their own families. And who do you want to go see? The grandchildren, of course! That means travel, which means even more money!

What if you live in the Northern States? How do you feel about staying up north all winter? For many, that answer is a big, fat NO! You may want to go south for the winter, maybe to Florida, Arizona, or Texas. Again, is it free to go south for the winter? I suspect you know the answer to that one.

What's It All Mean?

For almost everyone, you are fooling yourself if you think that you can get away with substantially less income in retirement. You may be able to live a comfortable retirement on a little less, but living on substantially less is usually a pipe dream. In fact, I would argue that a meaningful retirement requires MORE INCOME.

These are your Golden Years, the time where you have earned the right to retire in comfort and style. It's a time of living and not having to worry about whether you'll have enough money to do the things you want to do. Running out of money should never enter you mind. For this kind of retirement, you may very well need more income than ever before.

If you can't get by with substantially less income, what does that mean for your tax burden during retirement? You can certainly expect that your taxes will not be going down anytime soon.

Major Problem Number Two: Tax Rates in the Future Will Increase

For most of you, we don't even need to have this discussion. But I'll push on for those of you who are ignoring reality.

All you have to do is answer this simple question (I have lots of these in this chapter, don't I?): *Is the Federal Government really good at **spending less** money each year? How about this question: Has the Federal Government ever **spent less money** from one year to the next in recent memory?*

It doesn't matter what your political affiliation is. It doesn't matter which side of the aisle is in power. One thing you can bet your house on is that the government will spend more this year than they spent last year. It's not a matter of *will they*, it's a matter of **how much will they**.

Now, that might be OK if we can keep the growth rate of spending to a reasonable degree. But the problem is this tiny little part of our population known as the Baby Boomers. You've heard of these people, right? They are like the pig swallowed by a snake. If you look at the snake, you can see that pig go through the poor snake's body.

The first Baby Boomers are starting to reach retirement. And the problem with this is Social Security and Medicare. Thanks to the Baby Boomer generation, these two items in the Federal Budget will represent over half of the budget all by themselves before long. And it's just going to get worse.

In October 2006, the Associated Press reported the following:

*"Calculations by Boston University economist Lawrence Kotlikoff indicate that closing those gaps—$8 trillion for Social Security, many times that for Medicare—and paying off the existing deficit would require either **an immediate doubling of personal and corporate income taxes, a two-thirds cut in Social Security and Medicare benefits, or some combination of the two.**"*

Read that last part again: *"… an **immediate doubling** of personal and corporate income taxes, a **two-thirds cut** in Social Security and Medicare benefits, or some combination of the two."*

Quick, name the number one voting bloc in this country. It's people aged fifty-five and above. How many of them do you think are all excited about voting to reduce their Social Security and Medicare benefits by two-thirds, just so your taxes don't go up? How many of them, on the other hand, will likely be wildly in favor of raising your tax dollars so their benefits remain the same? Do you think the politicians know where these people, their number-one voting constituency, stand? You bet they do!

People complain about the deficit and the cost of the war in Iraq. But these numbers pale in comparison to the cost of Medicare and Social Security. Everyone knows that Social Security will be going broke before long, and the only solution is to either increase taxes or reduce benefits. Guess which one the voting public will choose? And remember, the voting public has never been really good with fiscal responsibility!

But the really bad news is in Medicare. Compared to Medicare, Social Security is on easy street. No one talks about Medicare, but it's on pace to be broke many years before Social Security.

Again, back to the same Associated Press article in October 2006:

> "Medicare already costs four times as much as it did in 1970, measured as a percentage of the nation's gross domestic product. And with the first baby boomers becoming eligible for Social Security in 2008 and for Medicare in 2011, the expenses of those two programs are about to increase dramatically due to demographic pressures. People are also living longer, which makes any program that provides benefits to retirees more expensive."

These two entitlement programs are in huge trouble already. What impact do you think the Baby Boomers will have? It's going to be a very ugly sight, and one that must lead to increased taxation!

An Historical Perspective

People don't realize how much lower our current tax rates are than they have been historically. Congress has a long history of taxing us at much higher levels. Figure 4-1 gives you an historical perspective of income tax rates.

Figure 4-1

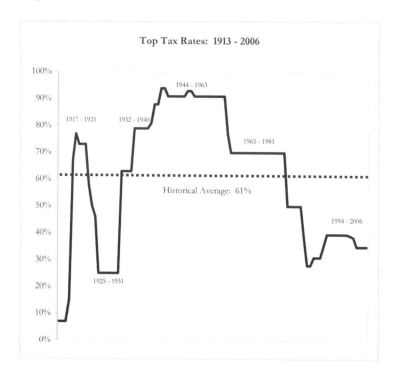

As you can see, we currently stand well below the historical averages, and Congress has been happy to raise tax rates in the past. As recently as the early 1990s, tax rates increased significantly, even though then-President George H.W. Bush (Bush senior) promised us, "Read my lips—no new taxes."

Summary

When we started this chapter, we talked about how all the experts argue that you should take your tax deduction today because you will likely be in a higher tax bracket right now then when you are retired.

By now, you should be convinced that it is unrealistic to expect to be in a lower tax bracket when you retire for two reasons. First, you will want to be at or above your pre-retirement standard of living. This means that your income will need to be the same as before retirement. Second, whether you want them to or not, the reality is that taxes are going up at some point down the road. Social Security and Medicare alone will require additional funding, and that doesn't even include other areas of government spending.

When all is said and done, you should think about your retirement this way: You will likely sacrifice, save and set aside money for twenty, thirty or forty years to have a comfortable retirement. If you can't retire at the same standard of living you are enjoying now, or even one a little bit better, what does that say for the job you did during the last twenty to forty years? That's a long time of saving to end up retiring to a life where you have to watch every penny. So if you end up in a comfortable lifestyle (as you should), taxes are going to have a substantially negative impact on your life. You need to assume that they will be there as a major obstacle to your retirement success.

CHAPTER 5

The Roth IRA

"A bend in the road is not the end of the road …
unless you fail to make the turn."

—*Anonymous*

So far, we've been discussing traditional retirement planning and why all the financial experts are so short-sighted. You may be wondering if you have any hope on the horizon.

Fortunately, you do, and it's called the Roth IRA. First available in 1998 and named after Senator William Roth from Delaware, the Roth IRA is the polar opposite of traditional retirement plans. You'll recall that with traditional retirement plans, you save tax on your seed, but your harvest is taxable. With a Roth IRA, it's just the opposite—you pay tax on your seed and your harvest is tax-free. So this sounds pretty good, right?

For the most part, it is pretty good. Unfortunately, remember how when the government giveth, it also taketh away? Just like traditional plans, Roth IRAs have several strings attached.

String Number One: Income Limitations

You can only contribute to a Roth IRA if your household adjustable gross income (AGI) falls below certain limits.

For a single taxpayer, it must be below $110,000. A single taxpayer has a phase-out for Roth IRA contributions for income between $95,000 and $110,000, which means that at $95,000, your ability to contribute begins to be limited.

For a married couple, your income must fall below $160,000, with phase-out limitations beginning at $150,000.

Now this may seem like some pretty big income numbers, and they are for most people. The point is that not everyone can contribute to a Roth IRA.

String Number Two: Investment Amount Limitations

Assuming that you qualify from an income perspective, your next limitation is the amount that you can invest into a Roth IRA each year. The rules are identical to a regular IRA.

As of this writing, an individual may contribute a maximum of $4,000 to a Roth IRA, or their adjusted gross income, whichever is smaller. If you are over the age of fifty, you can add in another $1,000, thus increasing your maximum annual contribution to $5,000, provided your earnings are larger than that.

String Number Three: Access to Your Money

Like traditional retirement plans, Roth IRAs are intended for retirement. The government has defined retirement age as no sooner than age 59½. That means you need to be over the age of 59½ to utilize the tax-free harvest of a Roth IRA to its full potential.

That being said, Roth IRAs have some different rules regarding accessing your account prior to age 59½.

First, the general rule with Roth IRAs is that when you make your first contribution to a Roth IRA, you begin a five-year waiting period. After the five years are over, you can then access the principal of your Roth IRA without tax.

During that five-year waiting period, you pay a 10 percent penalty if you withdraw money, unless you can satisfy one of the following criteria:

- You've reached age 59½.
- You are disabled.
- You died and the money is being paid to your beneficiary.
- You qualify for the "First-Time Home Purchase" rules.

As we've discussed before, other exceptions to the 10 percent penalty may apply to you and you should discuss this carefully with either your tax or financial advisor.

Comparing a Roth IRA to Traditional Retirement Plans

As I mentioned earlier, the primary difference of a Roth IRA is in the way it is treated from a tax perspective. Figure 5-1 shows you the differences in detail.

Once fully understood, many people who have accumulated assets in a traditional plan often desire to change to a Roth IRA. This can be completed (for most people) through a Roth IRA Conversion.

Roth Conversions

One of the unusual features of a Roth IRA is the ability to convert from a traditional retirement plan to a Roth IRA. The only restriction involves your adjusted gross income (AGI)—it must be less than $100,000. (Note: The $100,000 limit applies to individuals or married couples. You CANNOT convert if you are married, filing separately.) As long as your AGI is below $100,000, you can convert any amount of your traditional retirement plan into a Roth IRA.

Of course, you can't do this for free! You have to include the amount you convert in your income for the year. So if you convert

Figure 5-1

Feature	Traditional Retirement Plan	Roth IRA
Tax-Deductible Contributions	YES (Pre-Tax)	NO (After-Tax)
Tax-Advantaged Accumulation	YES (Tax-Deferred)	YES (Tax-Free)
Tax-Free Distributions	NO (Fully Taxable)	YES (Tax-Free)
Tax-Free Transfer To Beneficiaries	NO (Fully Taxable)	YES (Tax-Free)

$200,000 into a Roth IRA, then you will owe tax on an additional $200,000 of income. OUCH!

Another issue that sometimes comes into play is that you begin another five-year waiting period on the amount converted separately from any contributions you may have made previously. In other words, you can't touch the money converted for five years or you'll pay a penalty, unless you meet one of the exceptions discussed before.

The good news is that once you hit age 59½, these penalties no longer apply. So if you are converting after you turn 59½, there is no penalty at any point to access your money.

Back to John and Sara

By now, you are probably wondering how John and Sara would have benefited if they could have utilized a Roth IRA for their retirement planning, instead of a traditional plan. Let's take a look. Figure 5-2 outlines this scenario.

Remember, John and Sara are investing "after-tax" dollars, so there is a lot less money in this account than in the traditional retirement plan earlier. But the difference is that it is now 100 percent tax-free. The principal is accessible tax-free, the income is tax-free, and the children would inherit this account tax-free. Under current rules, this account could also be "Stretched" tax-free.

Let's assume that John and Sara wish to take distributions right away to enhance their retirement income. What would their income be? Again, assuming a 6 percent distribution rate:

- $752,680 × 6% =   **$45,161**

"Whoa, hold the fort there," you say. Isn't that the same number John and Sara had for after-tax income before with their traditional retirement plan? YES! And it should be in this example, because we are using the same tax rate throughout. But in our example, we are ignoring some very real life items.

First, we are assuming that taxes will NOT increase over time. From our last chapter, I hope that we can all agree that this is highly unlikely. If tax rates are higher down the road, then the income from John and Sara's previous analysis of their qualified plan would

Figure 5-2

Age Beg. Of Year	Age End Of Year	Beginning Balance	Annual Contribution	Less Tax Owed	8.00% Earnings	Ending Balance
30	31	$0	$6,000	$1,800	$168	**$4,368**
31	32	$4,368	$6,000	$1,800	$517	**$9,085**
32	33	$9,085	$6,000	$1,800	$895	**$14,180**
33	34	$14,180	$6,000	$1,800	$1,302	**$19,683**
34	35	$19,683	$6,000	$1,800	$1,743	**$25,625**
35	36	$25,625	$6,000	$1,800	$2,218	**$32,043**
36	37	$32,043	$6,000	$1,800	$2,731	**$38,975**
37	38	$38,975	$6,000	$1,800	$3,286	**$46,461**
38	39	$46,461	$6,000	$1,800	$3,885	**$54,546**
39	40	$54,546	$6,000	$1,800	$4,532	**$63,277**
40	41	$63,277	$6,000	$1,800	$5,230	**$72,707**
41	42	$72,707	$6,000	$1,800	$5,985	**$82,892**
42	43	$82,892	$6,000	$1,800	$6,799	**$93,891**
43	44	$93,891	$6,000	$1,800	$7,679	**$105,771**
44	45	$105,771	$6,000	$1,800	$8,630	**$118,600**
45	46	$118,600	$6,000	$1,800	$9,656	**$132,456**
46	47	$132,456	$6,000	$1,800	$10,765	**$147,421**
47	48	$147,421	$6,000	$1,800	$11,962	**$163,583**
48	49	$163,583	$6,000	$1,800	$13,255	**$181,037**
49	50	$181,037	$6,000	$1,800	$14,651	**$199,888**
50	51	$199,888	$6,000	$1,800	$16,159	**$220,247**
51	52	$220,247	$6,000	$1,800	$17,788	**$242,235**
52	53	$242,235	$6,000	$1,800	$19,547	**$265,982**
53	54	$265,982	$6,000	$1,800	$21,447	**$291,628**
54	55	$291,628	$6,000	$1,800	$23,498	**$319,327**
55	56	$319,327	$6,000	$1,800	$25,714	**$349,241**
56	57	$349,241	$6,000	$1,800	$28,107	**$381,548**
57	58	$381,548	$6,000	$1,800	$30,692	**$416,440**
58	59	$416,440	$6,000	$1,800	$33,483	**$454,123**
59	60	$454,123	$6,000	$1,800	$36,498	**$494,821**
60	61	$494,821	$6,000	$1,800	$39,754	**$538,775**
61	62	$538,775	$6,000	$1,800	$43,270	**$586,245**
62	63	$586,245	$6,000	$1,800	$47,068	**$637,512**
63	64	$637,512	$6,000	$1,800	$51,169	**$692,881**
64	65	$692,881	$6,000	$1,800	$55,599	**$752,680**
		Totals:	$210,000	$63,000	$605,680	

be taxed at higher rates, thus reducing the amount left over for spending. They would then end up with more money from using a Roth IRA.

Second, we are ignoring the fact that distributions from traditional retirement plans are counted in the equation when you determine how much of your Social Security income is taxable. Roth IRA distributions are not.

What does this mean? Often, traditional retirement plan distributions are taxed twice—once on the amount you distribute, *and again as you pay tax on Social Security income that you didn't have to pay tax on before the distribution.* We were NOT adding in any additional tax on Social Security income for John and Sara when we calculated their net income from their traditional retirement plans earlier.

The income from a Roth IRA, on the other hand, is ignored when it comes to calculating how much of your Social Security income is taxed. In fact, it is one of the very few sources of income that you can enjoy *without* affecting the tax on your Social Security income. Again, advantage—Roth.

Finally, Roth IRAs *have no required distribution.* This is huge for people who would prefer to keep their money in the plan until they decide to pull the money out, if ever. Since a Roth requires no distribution, it places full flexibility at your hands. If you want to take money out, do so with no tax. If you want to leave your money to grow tax-free, then do that. The choice is up to you with zero IRS interference.

Let's summarize the positive Roth IRA differences:

1. No impact on the level of taxation on your Social Security income.
2. Guaranteed zero tax down the road when taxes are almost certainly higher. Tax-free principal, tax-free income, and tax-free to children.
3. Complete freedom to withdraw money or not with no Required Minimum Distributions to worry about.

Even if the numbers end up being identical when John and Sara begin their retirement, they would clearly be in a far better and more flexible position by utilizing the Roth IRA in place of traditional planning.

So tell me again why the "experts" are right to use traditional plans? Seems to me like a whole bunch of people are making the mistake of not paying attention to the destination that their planning is taking them!

Summary

Roth IRAs offer a number of benefits that traditional retirement plans do not. Of particular importance is that with Roth IRAs, we finally get the result that we want with our retirement planning—a tax-free harvest!

Roth IRAs allow us to be smart about when we pay our tax, just like our story earlier of Farmer Brown. They allow us to pay tax on the small amount of seed (our contributions) so we can reap our harvest (retirement income) completely tax-free.

The only problem with Roth IRAs comes from converting a regular QRP to a Roth IRA, as you have to pay tax on the amount converted. This can be very large, depending on the size of your QRP.

As we go on to the next chapter, we're going to examine Roth conversions in more detail to see if we can learn whether they provide value and make sense.

CHAPTER 6

Roth Conversion

"A setback is the opportunity to begin again more intelligently."
—*Henry Ford*

In the last chapter, we learned about Roth IRAs and why they are so beneficial. Primarily, they allow you to enjoy a tax-free "harvest" of your money. In addition, they offer much more flexibility regarding distributions than other types of qualified plans (no required minimum, for example).

But for many of you, you already have built significant amounts in traditional IRAs, 401(k)s, 403(b)s, or other Qualified Retirement Plans (QRP). How can you benefit from a Roth IRA if you find yourself in this position?

Roth Conversion Basics

If you have a QRP, you may very well have the option of converting your QRP into a Roth IRA. In other words, you may have the option of converting from a taxable "harvest" to a tax-free "harvest." Doesn't that sound great?

Unfortunately, this is usually NOT a *cost-free* experience. You normally have to pay tax on the amount that you convert. For example, if you convert $100,000 of your 401(k) into a Roth IRA, you have to pay income tax on $100,000 *all in the year of conversion!* As you can imagine, this can be a pretty expensive tax.

And that's not all. You may not be able to convert to a Roth IRA *even if you are willing to pay the tax.* Why not? This is a very good question. Here are some simple rules about conversion:

1. No conversion is possible at all if your adjusted gross income (AGI), *not including the amount of conversion,* falls above $100,000 (again for an individual or a couple). You should be aware, however, that this rule is waived starting in 2010. (Don't you just love our tax code? Why 2010? Why not now?)

2. If your account is an IRA and your AGI is $100,000 or less, then you can convert any amount into a Roth IRA.

3. If your account is something other than a traditional IRA, like a 401(k) or 403(b) or 457, then you may have other rules that are specific to your plan that prevent a conversion.

4. If you are retired and you qualify under rule number one, then you can convert any amount into a Roth IRA, regardless of plan type.

That's pretty much it. The big problem with converting to a Roth IRA is not usually the lack of ability. It has a whole lot more to do with having to pay the tax on the amount you convert. But don't be dismayed! In future chapters, we are going to look into several ways you can convert to a Roth IRA (or something very similar) *without paying the tax*. At the very least, we'll learn if we can eliminate a big chunk of your tax liability!

For now, we first want to determine how you measure whether converting to a Roth IRA makes sense from a dollars-and-cents perspective.

Back to Joe and Carol

Do you remember Joe and Carol? They were the retirees I introduced you to at the very beginning of this book. Remember how mad they were because all their plans were in disarray due to the unexpected tax position they found themselves in? Let's see if we can go back and help them out a little bit.

Let's assume that Joe and Carol are both sixty-five years old and they want to actually use their QRPs for additional income during retirement. They have accumulated $500,000 in their QRPs and they are averaging 8 percent total earnings. Given today's life expectancies, we have to assume that at least one of them will make it to age eighty-five (and probably longer), so we'll investigate a twenty-year time horizon. Again, we'll use a combined 30 percent marginal tax rate for our analysis. Figure 6-1 shows what Joe and Carol can expect to see happen to them.

We see that Joe and Carol end up taking over $700,000 of income, but give back over $200,000 of it to the IRS. And when they die, their children stand to inherit $742,974 (also taxable), leading to another $200,000+ (at the 30 percent marginal tax rate) going to

Figure 6-1

Age Beg. Of Year	Age End Of Year	Beginning Balance	8.00% Earnings	6.00% Income	Tax Owed @ 30%	Cumulative Tax Paid	Ending Balance
65	66	$500,000	$40,000	$30,000	$9,000	$9,000	$510,000
66	67	$510,000	$40,800	$30,600	$9,180	$18,180	$520,200
67	68	$520,200	$41,616	$31,212	$9,364	$27,544	$530,604
68	69	$530,604	$42,448	$31,836	$9,551	$37,094	$541,216
69	70	$541,216	$43,297	$32,473	$9,742	$46,836	$552,040
70	71	$552,040	$44,163	$33,122	$9,937	$56,773	$563,081
71	72	$563,081	$45,046	$33,785	$10,135	$66,909	$574,343
72	73	$574,343	$45,947	$34,461	$10,338	$77,247	$585,830
73	74	$585,830	$46,866	$35,150	$10,545	$87,792	$597,546
74	75	$597,546	$47,804	$35,853	$10,756	$98,547	$609,497
75	76	$609,497	$48,760	$36,570	$10,971	$109,518	$621,687
76	77	$621,687	$49,735	$37,301	$11,190	$120,709	$634,121
77	78	$634,121	$50,730	$38,047	$11,414	$132,123	$646,803
78	79	$646,803	$51,744	$38,808	$11,642	$143,765	$659,739
79	80	$659,739	$52,779	$39,584	$11,875	$155,641	$672,934
80	81	$672,934	$53,835	$40,376	$12,113	$167,754	$686,393
81	82	$686,393	$54,911	$41,184	$12,355	$180,109	$700,121
82	83	$700,121	$56,010	$42,007	$12,602	$192,711	$714,123
83	84	$714,123	$57,130	$42,847	$12,854	$205,565	$728,406
84	85	$728,406	$58,272	$43,704	$13,111	$218,676	$742,974
		Totals:	$971,895	$728,921	$218,676		

Hypothetical only - no specific investment illustrated.

the IRS. So on this IRA that was valued at $500,000, Joe, Carol, and their children end up paying the IRS as follows:

- Joe and Carol: $218,676
- Children ($742,974 × 30%): <u>$222,892</u>
- Total tax paid: **$441,568**

As we learned earlier, if the children take advantage of "Stretch" provisions, the tax bill goes up. But isn't this interesting? Joe and Carol's QRP started at $500,000 and the IRS ended up collecting $440,000. What's the effective tax rate on that?

Now, let's take a little harder look at Joe and Carol's picture because that $440,000 tax bill may not be that low.

The Impact on Social Security Income

Depending on how their other retirement income is structured, Joe and Carol may be able to get away without paying tax on their Social Security income. QRP distributions, however, are included in the calculation that determines to what degree, if any, your Social Security income is taxable.

The sad result is that QRP distributions often make your Social Security income taxable. So Joe and Carol not only pay tax on their QRP distributions, they also may end up paying tax on their Social Security income as well. Talk about double taxation! And I did NOT include any additional tax on Social Security income in my analysis above.

Secondly, I am assuming that the tax rates for Joe and Carol will remain the same over the next twenty years. What do you think the odds are that taxes will remain the same ten, fifteen, or twenty years from now? After reading Chapter Four, I hope that you better understand the overwhelming likelihood that taxes will increase down the road.

What is the impact of increasing tax rates on Joe and Carol? It will obviously affect how much of their QRP distributions they will have left over to spend. But it may also have a significant impact on the potentially increased Social Security income that is taxed. For Joe and Carol, increased tax rates could hit them both ways in an ugly "double whammy."

Roth Conversion Benefits

What if Joe and Carol exercised their option to convert 100 percent of their QRPs to Roth IRAs right now? What would their tax bill be? Given our current tax structure, odds are high that they would end up paying a 40 percent tax (federal and state) on such a conversion. And 40 percent of $500,000 is a $200,000 tax! Talk about a kick in the pants!

> But here's the key question: *How long would they have to live before they would have to pay the IRS $200,000 anyway?*

It all depends on how you look at things. One set of people may take the perspective of keeping their tax liability to a minimum for the entire family. That means that they consider not just the taxes they pay, but also the taxes their children pay. If Joe and Carol find themselves in this group, then they would analyze a potential Roth Conversion like this:

- Tax paid on Roth Conversion: $200,000
- Total taxes paid without conversion: $441,568
- Benefit to family for conversion: $221,568

Joe and Carol would look at the above numbers and realize that when you factor in the whole family, Roth Conversion makes sense at any point, unless your account loses money in the investment markets. The reason for this is that all growth will be taxable to someone, either Joe and Carol or their children. So as long as their account grows at all, they never owe less tax than right now.

The other group of people are not as concerned about taxation on their children's inheritance. For them, the analysis is all about themselves, and not their children. Maybe they do not have any children. Or maybe their children are doing better financially than they ever did. Or maybe their value system is to not give a bunch of money to their children—make them stand on their own. Maybe the beneficiary of the account is a charity, so this money isn't going to family members anyway. Whatever the reason, they want to know how long they have to live for a Roth Conversion to break even *for them*.

69

Figure 6-1

Age Beg. Of Year	Age End Of Year	Beginning Balance	8.00% Earnings	6.00% Income	Tax Owed @ 30%	Cumulative Tax Paid	Ending Balance
65	66	$500,000	$40,000	$30,000	$9,000	$9,000	$510,000
66	67	$510,000	$40,800	$30,600	$9,180	$18,180	$520,200
67	68	$520,200	$41,616	$31,212	$9,364	$27,544	$530,604
68	69	$530,604	$42,448	$31,836	$9,551	$37,094	$541,216
69	70	$541,216	$43,297	$32,473	$9,742	$46,836	$552,040
70	71	$552,040	$44,163	$33,122	$9,937	$56,773	$563,081
71	72	$563,081	$45,046	$33,785	$10,135	$66,909	$574,343
72	73	$574,343	$45,947	$34,461	$10,338	$77,247	$585,830
73	74	$585,830	$46,866	$35,150	$10,545	$87,792	$597,546
74	75	$597,546	$47,804	$35,853	$10,756	$98,547	$609,497
75	76	$609,497	$48,760	$36,570	$10,971	$109,518	$621,687
76	77	$621,687	$49,735	$37,301	$11,190	$120,709	$634,121
77	78	$634,121	$50,730	$38,047	$11,414	$132,123	$646,803
78	79	$646,803	$51,744	$38,808	$11,642	$143,765	$659,739
79	80	$659,739	$52,779	$39,584	$11,875	$155,641	$672,934
80	81	$672,934	$53,835	$40,376	$12,113	$167,754	$686,393
81	82	$686,393	$54,911	$41,184	$12,355	$180,109	$700,121
82	83	$700,121	$56,010	$42,007	$12,602	$192,711	$714,123
83	84	$714,123	$57,130	$42,847	$12,854	$205,565	$728,406
84	85	$728,406	$58,272	$43,704	$13,111	$218,676	$742,974
		Totals:	$971,895	$728,921	$218,676		

Hypothetical only - no specific investment illustrated.

Looking at Figure 6-1 above, we learn that if Joe and Carol are part of this group, they must live to age eighty-three for a Roth Conversion to make sense. In other words, as long as they live to age eighty-three, they are better off converting to a Roth IRA than to pay tax each year on their distributions.

This is where a Roth Conversion decision becomes difficult. When you don't break even for eighteen years, that's a tough decision to make. I would likely advise against such a decision, unless you strongly believe tax rates will increase in the future, as I do. Later chapters will give you some options if you are in this position.

What if Joe and Carol Don't Spend Their Earnings?

That's a good question, isn't it? What if Joe and Carol don't need the earnings from their QRPs right now? What if they only take out their required minimum distributions? Isn't that what many people do anyway? Isn't that what all the experts say—keep on deferring as long as possible? If they aren't taking money out, then they aren't paying tax. Wouldn't a Roth Conversion be less attractive to them in that situation? Let's find out. Figure 6-2 details this scenario.

Here we learn that once again, if Joe and Carol consider both themselves and their children, a Roth Conversion makes sense from day one. The reason is the same: As long as the account is growing, it will never be cheaper to pay the tax than right now.

Figure 6-2

Age Beg. Of Year	Age End Of Year	Beginning Balance	8.00% Earnings	RMD Divisor	Required Distribution	Less Tax @ 30%	Cumulative Tax Paid	Ending Balance
65	66	$500,000	$40,000		$0	$0	$0	$540,000
66	67	$540,000	$43,200		$0	$0	$0	$583,200
67	68	$583,200	$46,656		$0	$0	$0	$629,856
68	69	$629,856	$50,388		$0	$0	$0	$680,244
69	70	$680,244	$54,420		$0	$0	$0	$734,664
70	71	$734,664	$58,773	27.4	$26,198	$7,859	$7,859	$767,239
71	72	$767,239	$61,379	26.5	$28,130	$8,439	$16,298	$800,488
72	73	$800,488	$64,039	25.6	$30,204	$9,061	$25,360	$834,323
73	74	$834,323	$66,746	24.7	$32,430	$9,729	$35,089	$868,639
74	75	$868,639	$69,491	23.8	$34,818	$10,445	$45,534	$903,312
75	76	$903,312	$72,265	22.9	$37,380	$11,214	$56,748	$938,197
76	77	$938,197	$75,056	22	$40,128	$12,038	$68,786	$973,125
77	78	$973,125	$77,850	21.2	$42,873	$12,862	$81,648	$1,008,102
78	79	$1,008,102	$80,648	20.3	$46,020	$13,806	$95,454	$1,042,730
79	80	$1,042,730	$83,418	19.5	$49,141	$14,742	$110,197	$1,077,008
80	81	$1,077,008	$86,161	18.7	$52,458	$15,737	$125,934	$1,110,710
81	82	$1,110,710	$88,857	17.9	$55,982	$16,795	$142,729	$1,143,585
82	83	$1,143,585	$91,487	17.1	$59,723	$17,917	$160,646	$1,175,349
83	84	$1,175,349	$94,028	16.3	$63,689	$19,107	$179,752	$1,205,688
84	85	$1,205,688	$96,455	15.5	$67,890	$20,367	$200,119	$1,234,253
				Totals:	$667,064	$200,119		

Hypothetical only - no specific investment illustrated.

On the other hand, if they have only themselves to consider, they don't break even until age eighty-four. Just like before, this is where a tough decision comes in, because that's a long time down the road for them.

If you look at this chart a little closer, you'll see that the tax liability for the family as a whole increases to a level significantly higher than before. A calculation of total tax paid now looks like this:

- Joe and Carol tax paid: $200,119
- Children tax paid ($1,234,253 × 30%): <u>$370,276</u>
- Total tax paid: **$570,395**

This is $130,000 more than before! How did this happen? In this scenario, Joe and Carol are compounding their QRPs much faster than before when they were taking income out of the accounts immediately. They were earning 8 percent, but taking income of 6 percent. This left the remaining 2 percent to compound within the QRP.

Now, they are compounding the entire 8 percent for the first five years. Then, they are distributing the minimum amount only, which starts out around 3.5 percent and slowly increases. A much greater portion of the earnings is reinvested and compounded when you take the minimum distributions only.

The Bottom Line

When you consider the tax on your entire family, a Roth Conversion, creating that tax-free "harvest," looks really attractive if you find yourself in retirement with regular QRPs. On the other hand, if you are in a position where you have only yourself to consider, then a Roth Conversion may have a very long break-even, perhaps as long as eighteen to twenty years.

When you are facing such a long break-even, you need to take a hard look at your life expectancy. If you are under the age of sixty and in reasonably good health, then you probably have enough time on your side to proceed with a Roth Conversion. But once you exceed the age of sixty, the time left to achieve break-even becomes a serious issue.

The good news is that in later chapters we'll learn about some creative ways you can make that conversion *without* paying all the tax to do so (or having someone else pay the tax for you), which may provide you an avenue, regardless of the position you find yourself in.

A Final Note

As you can imagine, the decision to convert from a regular QRP to a Roth IRA is a very big step. You should consider your circumstances very carefully before doing so and consult closely with either your CPA, Certified Financial Planner™ (CFP®), or trusted financial advisor before taking this step. Like all types of tax planning, you want to have a professional double check your thinking.

.

CHAPTER 7

Paying the Price of a Roth Conversion

"If a window of opportunity appears don't pull down the shade."
—*Tom Peters*

I n the last chapter, you were introduced to the idea of converting to a Roth IRA, even after retirement, to save substantially on future taxation. The primary downside was that, in our example, Joe and Carol had a nice big tax bill of $200,000.

I know that you think this is just pocket change, but Joe and Carol don't have that kind of money lying around. So we need to help them figure out how they can come up with money for the tax bill.

The good news is that, since Joe and Carol are over the age of 59½, they have the option of simply withdrawing the $200,000 from their new Roth IRA tax-free. Of course, that doesn't make it a good decision, but it is an option.

In this chapter, we're going to consider doing exactly that, but we're also going to think outside the box a little bit. We are actually going to look into doing something most of the so-called "experts" would consider completely crazy. We are going to investigate the possibility of using Joe and Carol's home equity to pay the tax on their Roth IRA conversion.

Using Home Equity

I know, I know! Using their home equity—am I crazy? They have their home paid for, how in the world could I even consider such a thing? After all, Joe and Carol are *retired*. What kind of financial planner would put a mortgage on their home at this point in their life?

Now that you have those questions out of your system, let's see where this path might lead. My job as a Certified Financial Planner™ is to investigate every possibility that may be worthwhile. And I believe that as we go down this path together, you'll begin to wonder why more people aren't open to the idea of utilizing their home equity in intelligent ways.

Home Equity—A Definition

Before we go too far, let's make sure that we are all starting in the same place. Some folks are not clear as to exactly what the "equity" in a home is. Here's a simple definition:

Home Equity = What Your Home Is Worth –
What You Owe on It

For example, if your home is worth $400,000 and your owe $150,000, then your home equity = $400,000 - $150,000 = $250,000.

It's an asset that you own. It's often just sitting there, doing a whole lot of nothing. Probably the biggest reason that people don't like to utilize their home equity has to do with what is known as "Depression Era Thinking," or DET.

Depression Era Thinking (DET)

You know people who suffer from DET and maybe you do yourself. A sure symptom of DET is operating under the assumption that "all debt is bad." I agree that much debt is bad, but all debt? I don't think so.

If all debt was bad, exactly how did pretty much every company in our country get started? How do they operate today? Look at almost any corporate balance sheet and what do you see? On the right hand side, you see something titled, "Liabilities." Do you know what liabilities are? Debt. Corporations use debt as a way to access other people's money and employ it to earn more than the cost of accessing that money.

How about banks? Every time you deposit money into a Certificate of Deposit (CD), guess what just happened? You "loaned" money to the bank. They "borrowed" it from you. Is that a dumb move on their part? Of course not! They take the money they borrowed from you and turn around and employ it to earn more than they have to pay for the use of your money. ***In other words, they use your money to get rich!*** Banks would be out of business if they couldn't borrow money from you, and others like you.

Now, as I mentioned a little bit earlier, I agree that much debt is bad. Fortunately, there exists an easy and straightforward way to determine if debt is good or bad. It works like this:

- Debt used to buy stuff that you don't really need = "Bad"
- Debt used to free up money to be employed to make more money = "Good"

That's pretty easy to figure out, isn't it?

Joe and Carol Using Home Equity to Pay the Tax on Roth Conversion

OK, let's see how this might work in practice. Remember, Joe and Carol need to come up with $200,000 to pay the IRS for converting their QRPs to Roth IRAs. Let's assume that they have a home with enough equity to pay the tax. In addition, we'll assume that they extract the equity from their home using an "interest-only" loan with a fixed rate of 7 percent. So their annual payments of interest-only are: $200,000 × 7 percent = $14,000 per year.

Now, what do we know about interest on a home? That's right, it's often tax-deductible. What does this do to the true cost of the loan? It reduces it by the amount of your annual tax savings. Since we are using a 30 percent rate in this book, Joe and Carol's true cost of the loan is calculated as follows:

- Annual loan payment: $14,000
- Less tax savings at 30%: $4,200
- Net cost of loan: $9,800

In other words, by taking out a loan, Joe and Carol *reduce* their annual tax bill by $4,200. So when you take that into account, they are only out $9,800, not the full $14,000. The result of this approach is found in Figure 7-1.

Now don't forget, Joe and Carol are NOT paying off any principal on their $200,000 loan, so when they die, their children will have to pay that off. From Figure 7-1, we see that the children will inherit a tax-free account worth $1,864,073. What do you think? Will the kids have enough money from the tax-free Roth IRAs to pay off the $200,000 loan?

This analysis looks pretty good, but how does it compare to just taking the taxes out of the IRA from the beginning?

Figure 7-1

Age Beg. Of Year	Age End Of Year	Beginning Balance	Amount Distributed	8.00% Earnings	Ending Balance
65	66	$500,000	$9,800	$39,608	$529,808
66	67	$529,808	$9,800	$41,993	$562,001
67	68	$562,001	$9,800	$44,568	$596,769
68	69	$596,769	$9,800	$47,349	$634,318
69	70	$634,318	$9,800	$50,353	$674,872
70	71	$674,872	$9,800	$53,598	$718,669
71	72	$718,669	$9,800	$57,102	$765,971
72	73	$765,971	$9,800	$60,886	$817,057
73	74	$817,057	$9,800	$64,973	$872,229
74	75	$872,229	$9,800	$69,386	$931,815
75	76	$931,815	$9,800	$74,153	$996,169
76	77	$996,169	$9,800	$79,301	$1,065,670
77	78	$1,065,670	$9,800	$84,862	$1,140,732
78	79	$1,140,732	$9,800	$90,867	$1,221,798
79	80	$1,221,798	$9,800	$97,352	$1,309,350
80	81	$1,309,350	$9,800	$104,356	$1,403,906
81	82	$1,403,906	$9,800	$111,920	$1,506,027
82	83	$1,506,027	$9,800	$120,090	$1,616,317
83	84	$1,616,317	$9,800	$128,913	$1,735,430
84	85	$1,735,430	$9,800	$138,442	$1,864,073
		Totals:	$196,000	$1,560,073	

Hypothetical only - no specific investment illustrated.

Taking the Money Out of the New Roth

We should also take a look at taking the $200,000 out of the Roth to pay the tax. After all, we don't want to pay that $9,800 bill the rest of our lives, right? Figure 7-2 explores this idea.

From Figure 7-2, we learn that the children inherit a little less than $1.4 million in this scenario. Let's compare the two:

- Using home equity: $1,664,073
- Paying tax from new Roth: $1,398,287
- Home equity advantage: **$265,786**

This is a pretty surprising result! In the first example, Joe and Carol take out a $200,000 loan to pay the tax. It's an interest-only loan—they aren't even paying a dime of principal.

This loan costs them a net $9,800 per year for the rest of their lives. If you add that up, that's $196,000 that they pay toward *interest*. And interest is a bad word, right?

But because they paid that $196,000 in interest, they ended up being $265,000 better off. Why? Because they took the equity from their home and *employed* it. In other words, they kept that money invested in the Roth and it grew at a faster rate than they were paying out.

This is very similar to the analysis we've had earlier on taking income from your QRPs versus RMDs only. The Roth IRA is earning 8 percent, but the distribution for the loan is at 5.1 percent. So the new

Figure 7-2

Age Beg. Of Year	Age End Of Year	Beginning Balance	Amount Distributed	8.00% Earnings	Ending Balance
65	66	$500,000	$200,000	$24,000	$324,000
66	67	$324,000	$0	$25,920	$349,920
67	68	$349,920	$0	$27,994	$377,914
68	69	$377,914	$0	$30,233	$408,147
69	70	$408,147	$0	$32,652	$440,798
70	71	$440,798	$0	$35,264	$476,062
71	72	$476,062	$0	$38,085	$514,147
72	73	$514,147	$0	$41,132	$555,279
73	74	$555,279	$0	$44,422	$599,701
74	75	$599,701	$0	$47,976	$647,677
75	76	$647,677	$0	$51,814	$699,492
76	77	$699,492	$0	$55,959	$755,451
77	78	$755,451	$0	$60,436	$815,887
78	79	$815,887	$0	$65,271	$881,158
79	80	$881,158	$0	$70,493	$951,651
80	81	$951,651	$0	$76,132	$1,027,783
81	82	$1,027,783	$0	$82,223	$1,110,005
82	83	$1,110,005	$0	$88,800	$1,198,806
83	84	$1,198,806	$0	$95,904	$1,294,710
84	85	$1,294,710	$0	$103,577	$1,398,287
		Totals:	$200,000	$1,098,287	

Roth has an extra 2.9 percent that can be reinvested to compound. But it gets even better.

You see, the interest-only loan is a payment that does not change. But the 2.9 percent reinvested is making the 8 percent earnings become a larger number over time. Here's what I mean …

	Roth Earnings	Interest Payment	Difference
Year 1:	$39,608	$9,800	$29,808
Year 5:	$50,353	$9,800	$40,553
Year 10:	$64,973	$9,800	$55,173
Year 15:	$97,352	$9,800	$87,552
Year 20:	$138,442	$9,800	$128,642

Doing What Banks Do

Joe and Carol are doing exactly what banks do. They used someone else's money (the bank's) and employed it to make more money than they had to pay for the use of the bank's money. In other words, they had to pay the bank a net 5.1 percent rate (after tax) to use their money while Joe and Carol were earning 8 percent tax-free. What a win for Joe and Carol!

Does Home Equity Earn a Rate of Return?

By now, most of you reading this are getting the idea. Using home equity to pay the tax on a Roth Conversion is better than using the Roth itself, *as long as you earn a higher rate of return inside the Roth than your after-tax cost of the loan.* This is exactly what banks do to get obscenely rich.

But some of you are saying to yourselves, "Wait a minute—you're not factoring in that my home is growing in value over time! Doesn't that loan reduce my future home earnings?" This is a common question, and you will soon learn that the answer is a resounding, "NO."

Think about it this way. Let's assume that Joe and Carol's home is worth $400,000. They are borrowing $200,000, and paying back interest only, no principal. Let's say that over time, their home grows in value from $400,000 to $600,000. What impact does this have on our analysis?

Well, if Joe and Carol did not take out a loan, and their home increases in value from $400,000 to $600,000, by how much does their net worth increase? Simple math says $200,000. But they took out a loan. What happens then?

Again, if their home increases from $400,000 to $600,000, by how much does their net worth increase? It's the same $200,000! It just doesn't matter how much equity they have in their home to start with, all that matters is that the home increases in value.

> **Home equity does NOT have a rate of return! The *value* of the home is what increases and is important, NOT the equity position!**

Summary

In this chapter, we looked at two ways to pay for a Roth Conversion—using the Roth itself, or tapping into your home equity with a fixed-rate, interest-only loan. We learned that while both results worked, using home equity to pay the tax worked the best.

I hope that this chapter helped you gain a wider perspective on using *all* of your assets to accomplish your objectives. Debt is not always bad, especially if you use it as the means to employ some of your assets to make more money than the costs that you incur.

By doing what the banks do, you have the opportunity to make your money work much harder for you and your family.

CHAPTER 8

Consider this "Investment"

"There is no security on this Earth, there is only opportunity."
—General Douglas MacArthur

In the last chapter, we stepped outside of the box and analyzed whether it would make sense to utilize the equity in Joe and Carol's home to pay the tax on a Roth Conversion. It turned out that this approach worked out very nicely.

In this chapter, we are going to step outside the box again to gain a different perspective. This chapter will take us on a little side trip, but we'll need this information for later chapters. So buckle up your seat belt and hang on!

Would You Be Interested in this "Investment"?

Let's assume that I am your financial advisor and I bring you a proposal to invest a substantial portion of your retirement money into an investment with the following characteristics:

1. You determine how much you will invest and for how long. Does this sound OK so far? Good!

2. You have the right to make extra contributions to your investment account any time you want—in fact, it's even encouraged. (Are you still OK with this investment? Great!)

3. Your investment account is not liquid. Getting money out of this account can sometimes be relatively easy, but can sometimes be impossible. (But that's OK, right? Isn't your QRP tied up to age 59½ anyway? This is retirement money.)

4. Your investment account starts out being pretty tax efficient, but as you go, each investment contribution reduces your tax efficiency. In fact, each year, your taxes increase. Can you live with that? (Probably as long as the returns are worthwhile, right?)

5. Your annual rate of return is guaranteed to be no more and no less than zero. (What?)

6. Every contribution you make to your investment account *reduces* the safety of your principal. (I must be kidding!)

7. After you fully fund your investment account based on the schedule you determined, your investment account provides you no income. (This is getting ridiculous, isn't it?)

8. Oh yes, last item—if you change your mind and don't pay into your account, or pay less than what you agreed to, the financial institution gets to keep your investment account. You get nothing!

OK, that's my "investment" proposal to you. How much do you want to invest in this account? How excited are you to put some big-time retirement dollars into this investment?

Of course, your answer is a big fat zero! You're not going to put one dollar into this so-called investment, are you? Who in their right mind would put any money into this type of investment anyway? What a ridiculous concept.

But here's the bad news: The sad fact is that millions of Americans are putting big-time money into exactly this investment. But they don't look at this investment in the way I've outlined above. They view it completely differently. And you know what this investment is that I'm describing. You know it by the names of "traditional mortgage" and "home equity."

But, But, But …

I know what you're thinking! You're saying, "Wait one minute! Stop right there! That's not how all the experts portray mortgages or home equity! Something must be missing here!"

I assure you that if you review each of the eight characteristics I described above, I am giving you a fair representation of traditional mortgages and the equity in your home. Why don't we cover each point in some detail, just to make sure we can see this from the same perspective.

Points One and Two: You Set the Schedule and You Can Pay More

This one is pretty easy. Whenever you take on a mortgage, you determine the schedule. Do you want a thirty-year mortgage or a fifteen-year mortgage? What about a twenty-year mortgage?

Do you want to make monthly payments? Bi-weekly? What amount of money do you wish to put into this program on a regular basis?

You determine all of this. You call the shots. And what does almost everybody recommend you do? You got it—pay a little extra every month.

If your scheduled payment is $950 per month, pay an even $1,000. If you can swing it, pay thirteen payments for the year instead of twelve. And that tax refund you just got—why not take some or all of that and pay it toward your principal? After all, think of all the interest you will save! Isn't that the kind of advice you hear all the time?

How many times have you heard, in conversation, people talking about paying extra on their mortgage? And everyone in the room agrees with them that this is the smart and prudent thing to do. Aren't they even a little smug about it?

But was it the smart and prudent thing for Joe and Carol to do in the last chapter? In fact, didn't Joe and Carol end up having hundreds of thousands of dollars *more* because they did just the opposite? They didn't pay any extra on their mortgage—they didn't even pay any principal!

By the end of this chapter, you will come to realize that the conventional thinking of paying down your mortgage at all, much less faster with extra payments, is *poison* to the disciplined investor!

Point Three: Lack of Liquidity

Many people just assume that the equity in their home is liquid and they can access it at any time. This, however, is pie-in-the-sky thinking and does NOT reflect any reality that you or I live in.

Think about it for a minute. How do you extract equity out of your home? You can choose one of two ways—you either sell your home or you get a loan. Can we all agree that selling a home for fair market value is often not an overnight event? In fact, the faster you need to get the money out of the home via a sale, the lower the price that you are likely to get.

So when you consider the equity in your home to be liquid, you are assuming that you can get a loan against it at any time. But is that really the case? As long as you have a steady income, and good credit, sure! But what about when times are bad?

Let me share a little story with you that happened to some friends of mine …

Ken and Linda

Ken and Linda (NOT their real names, of course) were doing everything "right." They bought their first home shortly after they married and took out a thirty-year traditional mortgage, and faithfully made every payment on time. In fact, every single month they paid in a little extra to pay that mortgage off early.

After several years of this, they also purchased a rental home, using the exact same approach. Life was good. They both had good jobs, and everything was flowing according to plan. But then, through no fault of his own, Ken hurt his back in an accident and couldn't work for several months, and a couple of weeks later, Linda got "downsized."

Of course, this happened when the economy wasn't doing so well and decent paying jobs were hard to find. And you know what happened next? The renters moved out and Ken and Linda had a hard time replacing them. What was the end result? They were unable to pay either mortgage, much less both of them.

But Ken wasn't too worried. He had a great relationship with the bank! After all, he had several years behind him of making payments on time, paying extra toward his principal every month, and generally being a dream customer for the bank.

He did some math and figured out that his extra payments over the years accumulated to the equivalent of two years' of regular payments. So he called the bank to let them know that due to their circumstances, they were going to suspend their payments for a while until things got back on track, and the bank should apply all those years of extra payments to his current payment for now. (I am NOT making this up! This is a true story.)

What do you think the bank's response to Ken's line of reasoning was? They shared with Ken that he could not use those extra payments in the past for today's payment. The system didn't work this way. The current payment was still due, and if Ken and Linda fell behind ninety days, then the bank would foreclose! As you can imagine, this came as a shock to Ken and Linda. After all, weren't they great customers? Didn't they make every single payment on time, and then some? They went from being the bank's "star customers" to being in the dog house in no time flat!

Well, Ken and Linda thought, they would just have to get a home equity loan to make the payments until they got back on their feet. So Ken called the bank back to make arrangements for a home equity loan. What did the bank tell him? You're right, they said, "Sorry, Ken." You can't even make your regular payments and you want us to loan you more money? Fat chance!

Because of their years of extra payments, Ken and Linda had over $250,000 of equity between their home and their rental unit. But how much of it could they get at? None! *What good did it do Ken and Linda to have $250,000 in real estate equity when they couldn't get at it?* They had just one option left. They had to sell. So they put both houses up for sale.

But remember, the economy was not doing so well, and houses weren't selling. They dropped their price, and dropped it some more, but neither home sold. As you can imagine, Ken and Linda started to panic. What in the world were they going to do?

Fortunately for Ken and Linda, their story had an OK ending. You see, Ken's parents inherited some money, and they loaned enough to Ken and Linda to tide them over. It wasn't the best solution, but it was good enough to get them through until Ken recovered and Linda found a new job.

Lesson Learned

What did Ken and Linda learn from their experience? What would you learn if you were them? Do you think that they've elected to pay even one dime more than their regularly scheduled mortgage payment since then?

How long do you think it took them (once they were back on their feet) to refinance and get that $250,000 of equity out of their real estate and put it somewhere they could get at it at any time?

Somewhere that was safe and truly liquid, that maybe even earned them a decent return?

How do they feel about their bank now? What happened to their nice warm and fuzzy feeling about their bank? Do you think that their bank is any different from any other bank? You know it isn't. They're all the same.

Ken and Linda should have never locked up their money in their real estate, even though all the experts say it's a good idea. Instead of making extra payments to reduce the principal of their loans, they should have put that money into a safe and liquid side account to grow and compound. Then, when times got tough, they would have had a resource that they could have drawn on to easily tide them over.

In fact, done properly, that safe and liquid side account would have grown to an amount large enough that they would have been able to pay off their home more quickly (if they chose) than the approach they were taking of paying down the principal directly!

What's the bottom line? Ken and Linda learned that home equity is liquid when times are good, but it's not liquid when times are bad. Tying up a huge chunk of money in your home equity will bite you when you least expect it. You must keep your assets liquid!

Can you call any account "liquid" if you can only get the money when you **don't** need it?

Point Four:
Each Payment Increases Your Tax Liability

If you think about this, you know why it's true. With a traditional mortgage, each year the interest you pay gets a little smaller and the principal portion of your payment gets a little larger. Which of the two do you get to deduct on your tax return? The interest only!

If your interest is getting smaller each year, what happens to the amount you get to deduct each year? It gets smaller too. If your deduction gets smaller each year, what happens to your taxable income? It goes up.

If your taxable income goes up, what happens to the taxes you owe? They go up. The net effect is that as you are paying down your mortgage, your tax deductions go down, which, in turn, makes your annual income tax liability increase.

To summarize:

- If your interest portion gets smaller, then ...
- Your tax deduction gets smaller, and if that happens ...
- Your net taxable income gets larger, which means ...
- Your tax liability gets larger.

Therefore, since each payment you make on a traditional mortgage reduces the interest portion of the next payment, then it follows that each payment you make *increases* your annual tax liability.

Point Five: Your Home Equity Earns a Guaranteed Zero Rate of Return

We covered this one in the last chapter, didn't we? You'll remember that Joe and Carol had a home worth $400,000. Remember how we said that if their home value increased to $600,000, that their net worth increased by $200,000?

Did it matter how much equity they had in their home? It didn't, did it? Whether the home was completely paid for, or 100 percent mortgaged, either way, their net worth increases by $200,000.

What does this mean? It means that home equity does not have a rate of return—it is equal to zero. Your *home* may increase in value, and that's what counts. The *equity* is simply a reflection of what's happening with your home's value.

Point Six: Payments Reduce the Safety of Your Principal

This one takes just a little bit of thinking. Let's use an example so we can get a clear picture of this concept.

Imagine two couples, the Smiths and the Joneses. They live next door to each other in identical homes both worth $400,000. Both Mr. Smith and Mr. Jones work together in the same job, and their company has laid them off and moved their jobs to India.

Neither Mr. Smith nor Mr. Jones can find a job, and they are way behind on their mortgage payments. There exists only one difference. The Smiths are just like Ken and Linda (who we discussed earlier). They've paid their mortgage down over the years with extra payments to a $150,000 balance.

The Joneses, on the other hand, have not paid one dime of principal. They took out an interest-only loan, and never paid more than the just the interest. In fact, over time as their home grew in value, they even increased their interest-only mortgage. Their mortgage balance stands at $350,000.

Since the big local company has moved all the jobs to India, many residents find themselves in a similar position. The housing market is flooded with homes for sale, so while their homes are worth $400,000, selling them at that price could take months, if not years. People are reducing home prices drastically to get their homes sold now.

You are the president of the bank that both the Smiths and the Joneses have their mortgages through. If you foreclose on them, you have to sell their home for enough money to pay off their loan. ***Who will you foreclose on first?*** *Will it be easier to sell the Smith's home for at least $150,000, or the Jones's home for $350,000?* (That's an easy one!)

You see, when you pay down your mortgage, you are increasing the safety of the bank's position. It becomes increasingly easier for the bank to foreclose and sell your home and get their money back.

If the bank's position is becoming increasingly safer over the years, what does that mean for your position? *It means that your position becomes increasingly riskier.*

What's the result? As you are paying down your principal, you are *reducing* your safety and *increasing* the bank's safety. It's no wonder that the banks push the idea that you should make extra payments on your mortgage. They want to get to a position of safety *for them* as quickly as possible.

Points Seven and Eight: No Income when Fully Funded and Bank Keeping Your Account

Let's say you make it to the point where your home is paid for. How much income will you receive in retirement from this account? Unless you sell your home and downsize, or take a reverse mortgage, the answer is a big fat goose egg! You get no income. You do get a whole bunch of money tied up in an asset earning nothing, but you don't get income.

Regarding the last point, we discussed it in the section before. If the bank forecloses because you don't make your payments, who keeps everything? Who loses everything? The bank wins and you lose. We all know that.

Summary

I began this chapter by telling you that I wanted to give you a different perspective. I hope that I've been able to accomplish this goal. There are very good reasons that all the big-time real estate owners don't tie up their money in their real estate. After this chapter, you should be able to see why.

Paying extra payments to your principal and tying up money in your home is a mistake! You earn nothing on that money and you can't get at it when you need to. Putting those extra payments into a safe and secure side account that you can access anytime you desire is a much smarter financial move.

That being said, it is a much smarter move only if you are *disciplined*. If you are not disciplined, then you will use your side account as a purchasing fund, and you will just end up with more stuff and no side account. That doesn't work! Be smart, and be disciplined, and you will profit handsomely.

A Final Note

You may be interested to know that in August 2006, the Federal Reserve Board of Chicago came out with a study that concluded the following:

> *"We show that a significant number of households can perform a tax arbitrage by cutting back on their additional mortgage payments and increasing their contributions in tax-deferred accounts (TDA)."*

"... U.S. households that are accelerating their mortgage payments instead of saving in tax-deferred accounts are making the wrong choice."

What are they saying? They are saying that ***you are better off to NOT pay down your mortgage***, and instead reallocate those dollars into traditional retirement plans. Even the Federal Reserve is telling you that making extra principal payments is the wrong thing to do!

Now think about this: If reallocating those dollars into traditional retirement plans makes sense, imagine how much more sense it would make to reallocate those dollars into the planning that we'll be discussing throughout the rest of this book. Pay close attention, as your opportunities are large!

CHAPTER 9

The "IRA Tax Rescue Plan"

"In the middle of difficulty lies opportunity."
—Albert Einstein

In the last chapter, we took a step outside the box of traditional thinking by taking a fresh look at how your home equity stacks up as an investment. In previous chapters, we looked at different ways we could convert Joe and Carol's QRPs to Roth IRAs to learn if it made sense. The bad news was that even if it made sense, we still had to pay a bunch of tax.

In this chapter, we're going to take another step or two to see if we can create a strategy to help Joe and Carol get out of the taxable predicament they are in and help them create a tax-free harvest of their retirement plan accounts. And we will look into ways of doing that *without* owing tax on the transition.

Before we begin this chapter, however, I need to give you fair warning—*the concepts discussed within this chapter represent a significant change from traditional thinking.* We are attempting to create a result that "most people" do not achieve, that is, distributing assets out of QRPs *without* paying tax. Then, we want to reposition those assets into *tax-free* accounts for Joe and Carol's future use.

It's been said that the definition of insanity is "doing the same thing over and over and expecting different results." If we want to get results that are different than what everyone else gets, we need to do something different. This chapter covers how to be different in an intelligent way so you can extract QRP dollars *without* the tax.

Joe and Carol—Current Circumstances

If you remember, Joe and Carol have QRPs totaling $500,000. This represents a taxable account, and every dollar they take out will be taxable. Why don't we see if we can help Joe and Carol keep their taxes to a minimum?

We'll cover two scenarios. This chapter will cover the first, in which we'll assume that Joe and Carol desire to take income out of their QRPs for retirement. In a later chapter, we will discuss what we can do when they are planning to only take out their required minimum distributions.

Again, we'll maintain our assumptions that we've been using throughout the book of a 30 percent marginal tax bracket, 8 percent earnings, and a life expectancy to age eighty-five. We'll also assume that we reinvest some of the income to address future inflation.

The first scenario, taking income, is shown in Figure 9-1.

Now, let's look at the tax implications. Joe and Carol take out a total of $728,921. At our marginal tax rate of 30 percent, they owe tax of $218,676. In addition, their children receive a taxable inheritance of $742,974. Again using our marginal tax rate of 30 percent, then they owe tax of $222,892. So let's sum this up:

- Tax paid by Joe and Carol: $218,676
- Tax paid by children: $222,892
- Total tax paid: $441,568

Over $440,000 of tax on a retirement plan that was worth $500,000! What does that tax rate work out to be? No matter how you look at it, that's a pretty large slice going to the IRS. What could we do to help them out?

A Different Idea

To help Joe and Carol, we need to make sure that we are considering using *all* of their assets. Remember, Joe and Carol are sitting on a home worth $400,000 that is completely paid for. Could we

Figure 9-1

Age Beg. Of Year	Age End Of Year	Beginning Balance	8.00% Earnings	6.00% Distribution	Less Tax	Net Income	Taxable Balance
65	66	$500,000	$40,000	$30,000	$9,000	$21,000	$510,000
66	67	$510,000	$40,800	$30,600	$9,180	$21,420	$520,200
67	68	$520,200	$41,616	$31,212	$9,364	$21,848	$530,604
68	69	$530,604	$42,448	$31,836	$9,551	$22,285	$541,216
69	70	$541,216	$43,297	$32,473	$9,742	$22,731	$552,040
70	71	$552,040	$44,163	$33,122	$9,937	$23,186	$563,081
71	72	$563,081	$45,046	$33,785	$10,135	$23,649	$574,343
72	73	$574,343	$45,947	$34,461	$10,338	$24,122	$585,830
73	74	$585,830	$46,866	$35,150	$10,545	$24,605	$597,546
74	75	$597,546	$47,804	$35,853	$10,756	$25,097	$609,497
75	76	$609,497	$48,760	$36,570	$10,971	$25,599	$621,687
76	77	$621,687	$49,735	$37,301	$11,190	$26,111	$634,121
77	78	$634,121	$50,730	$38,047	$11,414	$26,633	$646,803
78	79	$646,803	$51,744	$38,808	$11,642	$27,166	$659,739
79	80	$659,739	$52,779	$39,584	$11,875	$27,709	$672,934
80	81	$672,934	$53,835	$40,376	$12,113	$28,263	$686,393
81	82	$686,393	$54,911	$41,184	$12,355	$28,828	$700,121
82	83	$700,121	$56,010	$42,007	$12,602	$29,405	$714,123
83	84	$714,123	$57,130	$42,847	$12,854	$29,993	$728,406
84	85	$728,406	$58,272	$43,704	$13,111	$30,593	$742,974
	Totals:		$971,895	$728,921	$218,676	$510,245	

Hypothetical only - no specific investment illustrated.

potentially use this asset in an intelligent way to help Joe and Carol with their huge future tax liability?

What If?

What if we have Joe and Carol take out a loan against their home for $300,000? What if this loan was structured in such a manner where they paid the interest only? What if that interest rate was fixed for the next fifteen years? What if we had Joe and Carol pay this loan with additional distributions from their retirement plans?

What if we then took the money that was extracted from the home ($300,000) and invested it into a safe, liquid side account that had some really interesting tax advantages? What if this side account allowed them to invest the $300,000 in an account that enjoyed tax-free growth, tax-free distributions, and tax-free transfer to named beneficiaries?

What kind of result might Joe and Carol expect from such a planning approach? Could they realize a significant and substantial benefit? Let's find out!

The "IRA Tax Rescue Plan"

Before we jump into the numbers, let's take a minute to discuss exactly the approach that I am describing.

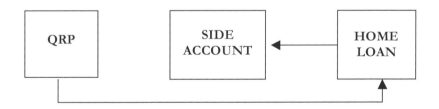

STEP ONE: Home loan is taken out for $300,000 on an interest-only basis. This means that *only the interest* will be paid and NOT the principal. Why? Because interest is usually deductible on your tax return, but principal is not. Assuming a 7 percent rate (typical as of this writing), the annual deductible interest payment equals $21,000 per year.

STEP TWO: Take additional distributions out of the QRP to pay the interest payment. This will lead to a tax-free distribution of the additional amount out of the QRP. Why? Because the QRP additional distribution of $21,000 is normally taxable, *but it is completely offset by the deduction of the interest!* (Note: Please consult your tax advisor to determine if the interest payment would be fully deductible for you, as this may not always be the case.)

STEP THREE: Invest the proceeds from the home loan into a safe, liquid side account that offers multiple tax advantages (similar to a Roth IRA, if possible). We'll discuss this in more detail later in this chapter.

Back to Joe and Carol

Now, let's go back to Joe and Carol. You might remember that we were discussing a plan where they take out an interest-only mortgage, pay the mortgage with additional QRP distributions, and invest the mortgage proceeds into a safe and liquid side account with tax advantages. Let's see how this might work out.

CLEAR THINKING

Many people initially close their minds to this concept because they feel very comfortable having their home "paid for." This makes them feel secure, and they feel that even if they spend all of their money over their lifetime, they'll always have a place to live and their children will at least inherit the home. The system I've just described repositions the equity from being in the home (where it earns nothing) and places it somewhere safe where it can earn a positive rate of return, greater than the cost of the loan.

If you are someone who feels secure about having your home paid for, then this planning, provided you are financially disciplined, should make you feel *even more secure.*

Think about it—what is the difference between having a home paid for versus having a mortgage combined with a side account that is large enough to pay off the mortgage any time you want? Only one thing. The person with the side account has a much greater degree of liquidity and flexibility than the person who has their equity locked in their home.

What if you need the money locked in your home for some reason? Maybe a child has a health emergency, which requires immediate financial assistance. Or maybe a natural disaster strikes, like a flood or tornado or fire that destroys your home. Having your equity positioned in a safe, liquid side account can be the difference between having flexibility and options versus heartache. Just ask someone who suffered through Hurricane Katrina.

We first need to learn what kind of impact these additional mortgage distributions will have on Joe and Carol's QRPs. Figure 9-2 illustrates this scenario.

Figure 9-2

Age Beg. Of Year	Age End Of Year	Beginning Balance	8.00% Earnings	6.00% Distribution	Plus Home Loan Pymt.	Total Distribution	Taxable Balance
65	66	$500,000	$40,000	$30,000	$21,000	$51,000	$489,000
66	67	$489,000	$39,120	$30,600	$21,000	$51,600	$476,520
67	68	$476,520	$38,122	$31,212	$21,000	$52,212	$462,430
68	69	$462,430	$36,994	$31,836	$21,000	$52,836	$446,588
69	70	$446,588	$35,727	$32,473	$21,000	$53,473	$428,842
70	71	$428,842	$34,307	$33,122	$21,000	$54,122	$409,027
71	72	$409,027	$32,722	$33,785	$21,000	$54,785	$386,964
72	73	$386,964	$30,957	$34,461	$21,000	$55,461	$362,461
73	74	$362,461	$28,997	$35,150	$21,000	$56,150	$335,308
74	75	$335,308	$26,825	$35,853	$21,000	$56,853	$305,279
75	76	$305,279	$24,422	$36,570	$21,000	$57,570	$272,132
76	77	$272,132	$21,771	$37,301	$21,000	$58,301	$235,601
77	78	$235,601	$18,848	$38,047	$21,000	$59,047	$195,402
78	79	$195,402	$15,632	$38,808	$21,000	$59,808	$151,226
79	80	$151,226	$12,098	$39,584	$21,000	$60,584	$102,740
80	81	$102,740	$8,219	$40,376	$21,000	$61,376	$49,583
81	82	$49,583	$3,967	$41,184	$21,000	$53,550	$0
82	83	$0	$0	$42,007	$21,000	$0	$0
83	84	$0	$0	$42,847	$21,000	$0	$0
84	85	$0	$0	$43,704	$21,000	$0	$0
	Totals:		$448,728	$728,921	$420,000	$948,728	

Total Taxable Distributions: $528,728

Hypothetical only - no specific investment illustrated.

Here we see that we have good news and bad news for Joe and Carol. The good news is that we are able to reduce their taxable distributions from $728,921 down to $528,728. This is a reduction of roughly $200,000. So Joe and Carol experience the following tax savings:

- Previous tax bill: $728,921 × 30% = $218,676
- New tax bill: $528,728 × 30% = $158,618
- Tax savings for Joe and Carol: **$60,058**

In addition, at their death, there is no money left in the QRP, so their children's tax liability goes to zero. Remember, the children would have had a tax bill of $222,892. Now they don't owe any tax, so their tax savings is 100 percent. Let's see how the total taxation on Joe and Carol's QRPs work out now:

- Previous tax bill—Joe and Carol: $218,676
- Previous tax bill—children: $222,892
- Previous tax bill—total: $441,568

- New tax bill—Joe and Carol: $158,618
- New tax bill—children: $0
- New tax bill—total: $158,618

- **Total tax savings:**   **$282,950**

The good news here is that Joe, Carol and their family save $282,950 of tax using the IRA Tax Rescue Plan. Unfortunately, we also have some bad news as well.

The bad news is that Joe and Carol's QRPs run out of money about the time they are eighty-two years old. This causes some problems for two reasons. First, they want around $30,000 after tax to live on (see Figure 9-1). Second, they still have a $300,000 loan, which requires a $21,000 payment (still tax deductible). And they have no QRP money left to fund either one!

But what do they have now that they didn't have before? That's right—they have the side account that was invested and has been growing all these years. So where did Joe and Carol invest that money? They did something that most people wouldn't have even considered—they invested the home equity proceeds into something called "Maximum Funded Equity Indexed Universal Life Insurance."

Maximum Funded Equity Indexed Universal Life Insurance

Wow, talk about taking a step outside of the box! I think we can all agree that putting the home equity proceeds into life insurance was about the last thing that would have come to your mind. This is definitely different from what "most people" would do!

So why in the world did Joe and Carol put their home equity into life insurance? And what is this type of insurance anyway? If you are like me, you've probably heard that life insurance is a "lousy" investment, so how can this possibly be a good idea?

To understand why this type of insurance might work so well in this application, we need to have a better understanding of some of the unique features that life insurance provides. And we need to better understand how this type of insurance is structured, and how it differs from what you and I traditionally think about when it comes to life insurance.

Historically, you and I probably grew up thinking about life insurance as a way to financially protect our families if we were to die at an early age. The idea was that we would attempt to get as *large of a death benefit* as we could at the *smallest possible cost*.

We didn't really care about "cash values" or some of the more arcane tax benefits that those cash values had. All we really cared about was how much death benefit could we obtain for how little cost. We knew that the death benefit was tax-free and that was about as far as it would go.

Your insurance agent might have talked you into "permanent" policies that grew some small amounts of cash value. You could use that cash value at any age for any reason, but you often had to borrow it from yourself and it was probably pretty confusing. If you had that type of policy, odds are high that it didn't earn the types of returns that you expected, thus it ended up being a lousy investment.

So how are these Maximum Funded Equity Indexed policies any better? This is a very good question, and is best answered by reviewing some not too distant history.

A Brief History

Think back to the 1970s. Do you remember what the top tax brackets were? You can go back and look at Figure 4-1 in Chapter Four, if you'd like. They were 70 percent! Now imagine that you were a corporate executive during this time period and had an investment portfolio of $500,000. This was before most retirement plans, so odds are that your portfolio was just a regular portfolio, subject to taxation each year.

Imagine that each year you would earn a return on this portfolio. Guess what tax rate was often applied to your earnings? That's right—70 percent! If you see 70 percent of your earnings vanish to the IRS every year, what are you screaming at your investment advisor to help you do? Obviously, tax avoidance becomes a major factor in your investment planning.

So along comes a little company you may have heard of, E.F. Hutton. They came up with the idea of investing your $500,000 into a life insurance plan. You see, life insurance cash values have always enjoyed tax-free growth, tax-free death benefits, and tax-free distributions during your lifetime, assuming that you take the money out properly. Simply put, all of your contributions come out tax-free first, and then your earnings can be distributed tax-free via a loan arrangement where you basically borrow from yourself. (It may sound a little goofy, but it works really well in practice.)

But E.F. Hutton's clients weren't really looking for life insurance. They normally had all kinds of life insurance. They were just looking for a way to avoid taxation (just like how a Roth IRA works today). Since insurance costs are based on the amount of coverage, the goal ended up being *how small of a death benefit could you have*. The smaller the death benefit, the smaller the costs, and the bigger the tax-free returns.

So it ended up being common practice at the time to have a token amount of insurance coverage, say $10,000. And these big executives would make a single investment of $500,000 into a life insurance plan with a $10,000 death benefit. What a deal! The $500,000 earned tax-free interest (about 15 percent in those days!) and the only cost was the insurance cost on a $10,000 policy, maybe a couple of hundred bucks.

From the perspective of the corporate executives, it was either pay tax on the earnings (up to 70 percent) or pay a couple of hundred bucks toward insurance costs. This was a really easy decision.

As you can imagine, all good things must come to an end, and the IRS caught wind of this. However, the IRS was in a bit of a pinch, because this plan was completely legal under the tax rules of the day. So the IRS went to Congress to get them to change the rules. As a result, two laws were passed, one in 1982—the Tax Equity and Fiscal Responsibility Act of 1982 (TEFRA)—and one in 1984—the Deficit Reduction Act of 1984 (DEFRA). Among the many things that these laws addressed were these types of investment/insurance plans. The bottom line was that TEFRA and DEFRA defined how much death benefit a person had to have in comparison to the dollars they invested.

For example, a sixty-five-year-old male in decent health investing $500,000 might be forced to have, at a minimum, $1 million of life insurance, instead of $10,000. As you can imagine, the costs are much higher for $1 million than for $10,000. That being said, the costs for $1 million worth of coverage were still peanuts compared to the alternative of paying taxes, so these plans continued to prosper.

In fact, these tax laws made these types of plans even *more* popular. Prior to these tax laws, many corporate executives shied away from these plans because they were concerned that sheltering $500,000 of investments under a small $10,000 life insurance plan was "too good to be true." They were worried that Congress would catch on and retroactively punish the people who took advantage of this tax loophole.

So what did Congress do to all the people who invested under the prior arrangement? It turns out that they were "grandfathered" in. That meant that the government basically said that if you did this type of plan in the past, you're OK. You just couldn't do it any more. *From this day forward,* you have to have a reasonable death benefit for the amount of money you invest.

But it was still such a great deal that the IRS wasn't happy with the result. Yes, these corporate executives had to have a lot bigger death benefit, but the costs of those larger death benefits still paled in comparison to the cost of taxes on their investments.

So the IRS pressured Congress to make these plans a little less attractive yet. And in 1988, Congress passed the Technical and Miscellaneous Revenue Act of 1988 (TAMRA). TAMRA was another big tax law change (like TEFRA and DEFRA), and a small part of TAMRA addressed these insurance plans by identifying a "contribution period." TAMRA said that if you want your insurance cash values to be accessible tax-free, then you had to fund the plan over a minimum of five years (called, in the logic of Congress, the seven-pay test).

This funding period had a definite impact on the attractiveness of these types of plans! From an investment perspective, until these plans are fully funded, they are not the most attractive investment. So you have to go through the "short-term pain" to get to the "long-term gain."

Of course, there does exist one way that these plans can be an excellent investment in the early years. If you happen to die early, your beneficiary (usually your spouse or children) realizes a ridiculously large rate of return on your investment—completely tax-free! The only problem, of course, is that you are not around to enjoy it with them.

But let's get back to our discussion. Once TAMRA was passed, previous plans were grandfathered in just like before. And since then, no more laws have been passed that impact these types of insurance plans.

To recap, today we have a minimum amount of death benefit required based on someone's age and health (TEFRA and DEFRA), and we have a minimum time period of five years to fund these plans (TAMRA).

Back to Joe and Carol

Figure 9-3 shows you what this looks like for Joe and Carol. We put the life insurance on Joe with Carol as the primary beneficiary, as wives normally outlive their husbands. We figured that if Joe died and left Carol some extra money tax-free, she would be OK with that. Carol agreed that this would certainly be OK, and that if Joe didn't behave himself, perhaps Carol would collect the proceeds a little sooner rather than later.

Figure 9-3

Age Beg. Of Year	Age End Of Year	Premium	Cash Value	Surrender Value	Death Benefit	Cash Flow	Net Death Benefit
65	66	$63,600	$61,426	$32,527	$628,247	$0	$328,247
66	67	$63,600	$127,376	$98,477	$628,247	$0	$328,247
67	68	$63,600	$198,200	$169,301	$628,247	$0	$328,247
68	69	$63,600	$274,603	$245,704	$628,247	$0	$328,247
69	70	$63,600	$357,281	$328,382	$628,247	$0	$328,247
70	71	$0	$381,468	$355,170	$628,247	$0	$328,247
71	72	$0	$407,474	$383,777	$628,247	$0	$328,247
72	73	$0	$435,585	$414,488	$628,247	$0	$328,247
73	74	$0	$465,965	$447,470	$628,247	$0	$328,247
74	75	$0	$501,350	$485,456	$628,247	$0	$328,247
75	76	$0	$539,987	$526,982	$628,247	$0	$328,247
76	77	$0	$582,389	$571,985	$628,247	$0	$328,247
77	78	$0	$628,851	$621,048	$660,294	$0	$360,294
78	79	$0	$679,219	$674,017	$713,180	$0	$413,180
79	80	$0	$733,748	$731,147	$770,435	$0	$470,435
80	81	$0	$792,477	$792,477	$832,101	$0	$532,101
81	82	$0	$846,766	$846,766	$889,566	$8,634	$589,566
82	83	$0	$867,644	$867,644	$913,878	$44,105	$613,878
83	84	$0	$890,139	$890,139	$940,086	$44,693	$640,086
84	85	$0	$914,385	$914,385	$968,346	$45,293	$668,346
		$318,000				$142,725	

Typical Maximum Funded Equity Indexed Universal Life Insurance Plan - 65 Year Old Male, Good Health.

The columns in Figure 9-3 are pretty self-explanatory for the most part. It may be helpful, however, to review how the premiums and cash flow numbers were calculated.

Calculating Premiums

In Figure 9-3, we see that the premiums come to $63,600 per year, totaling $318,000 after five years. Yet we are only taking out $300,000 of home equity to be repositioned. What accounts for the difference?

It's really pretty simple. Due to TAMRA, we cannot put all $300,000 in the insurance plan immediately or we lose our tax-free withdrawal benefits. If you recall, we need to spread out the investment over five years.

So in the first year, we put $63,600 into the insurance plan. That leaves us $236,400 to invest outside of the insurance plan until next year's premium comes due. We don't want to risk this money, so we will typically create a CD or Government bond ladder.

If you are unfamiliar with CD and bond ladders, Figure 9-4 shows you the details of such a program. You can also use an immediate annuity to transition the $300,000 into the life insurance.

Calculating Withdrawal Amounts

Let's start with Joe and Carol's withdrawal of $44,105. This represents the first year that they must take money out of their side

Figure 9-4

	Amount Invested	End Of Year 1	End Of Year 2	End Of Year 3	End Of Year 4
Immediate Premium	$63,600				
1 Year CD	$61,748	$63,600			
2 Year CD	$59,949	$61,748	$63,600		
3 Year CD	$58,203	$59,949	$61,748	$63,600	
4 Year CD	$56,508	$58,203	$59,949	$61,748	$63,600
Totals:	$300,007	$243,500	$185,297	$125,348	$63,600

Assumes an after-tax 3% rate of return.
Hypothetical only - no specific CD or Government Bond illustrated.

account because they fully exhausted their QRPs. From Figure 9-1, we see that the net, after-tax income that Joe and Carol wanted was $29,405. Remember, insurance distributions are tax-free, so we can distribute that $29,405 without subtracting additional taxes.

But we still have the mortgage interest payment to account for. We need to determine the after-tax value of the interest payment, so we can stay consistent.

- Interest payment: $21,000
- Less tax deduction benefit at 30%: $6,300
- Net interest payment: $14,700

- Plus income needs: $29,405
- Total amount needed to withdraw: **$44,105**

The last two years of Joe's life are calculated in a similar fashion. For the partial distribution in the first year of $8,634, I simply took the shortfall from Figure 9-2 as follows:

- Income needed: $41,184
- Mortgage payment: $21,000
- Total income needed: $62,184
- Less income available ($49,583 + $3,967): $53,550
- Shortfall: **$8,634**

The other columns that may need discussion are the cash value column and the surrender value column. The cash value column represents the combination of the following:

- Premiums paid in
- Plus earnings
- Less insurance costs

The surrender value is the portion of the cash value that you would receive if you were to discontinue the insurance plan and cash it in. You normally would not receive your entire cash value if you were to discontinue the program in the first several years. The difference is referred to as a "surrender charge" and it compensates the insurance company for the costs they incur when you discontinue a plan in the early years.

Insurance companies invest the money you put into these plans on a long-term basis. This allows them to earn higher returns than is typical for safe investments. Obviously, if they have to cash in early, they would pay a penalty, and they pass that on to you.

You can find maximum funded insurance plans that have no surrender charge, or that credit large cash values in early years. Remember that everything comes at a price. If you receive positive benefits early on, what do you think will happen in later years? Always look at long-term results! Early benefits come at a price, and often a big one.

Plan Benefits

First, we see that the children stand to inherit significantly more money than before. If you remember, before they were going to inherit a *taxable* account of $742,974. After we account for a 30 percent tax hit (again, we're assuming a much lower rate than they would pay on that amount of money), they would have the following:

- Taxable inheritance: $742,974
- Less 30% tax: $222,892
- After-tax inheritance: **$520,082**

Now, the entire account is *tax-free* money, so it is tax-free to the children. So how much better off are they?

- Tax-free net death benefit: $668,346
- Previous taxable inheritance: $520,082
- Net benefit of planning: **$148,264**

So Joe and Carol enjoy the same income with less tax and their children end up with more money as a result. This is a classic win/win!

But what if Joe and Carol decided that they wanted to spend more money on themselves instead of leaving more to their children? Could they choose to do that?

You bet they can! In fact, this is exactly what I recommend. Look at how much tax-free cash they have to spend on anything they want once their insurance plan is fully funded—$328,382. That's a lot of money to enhance their retirement lifestyle! And they can use it whenever, and for whatever, they want, and it's all tax-free.

The downside is that if they take some money out of this account, they reduce the tax-free death benefit. For example, if they take out $100,000 to spend on a world-wide vacation spree for the next two years, the death benefit is reduced by $100,000. So what?

So their children get $100,000 less—that's because Joe and Carol spent it. Whose money is it anyway? In fact, in this case, Joe and Carol's children were almost $150,000 better off because of this plan. If Joe and Carol spend that $100,000, then the children are still $50,000 better off. Bottom line, the kids *still* get more money!

But can you imagine how much Joe and Carol could do with that extra $100,000? Can you imagine how much that could enhance their Golden Years?

Summary

In this chapter, we assumed that Joe and Carol wanted to actually spend their earnings during their retirement years. The problem that they were facing was one of enormous taxation.

By utilizing the IRA Tax Rescue Plan, we were able to save Joe, Carol and their family $282,950 of tax, create a huge bucket of tax-free cash for Joe and Carol to use for whatever they want, and deliver more money to their children tax-free all at the same time. This is what I like to call making a significant and substantial benefit for Joe and Carol during their retirement!

When all is said and done, we are talking about your money and your assets. If you take advantage of the opportunities in front of you, you can often create a meaningful, positive difference in your own lives. Many of you reading this have the same opportunities as Joe and Carol, you only have to reach out and grab them.

Think about the possibilities! If you want to take an extra trip each year, do it. If you want a new car, buy it. If you want to take your grandchildren to Disney World, plan it. If you want to contribute more to your church or favorite charity, then do so. You can even take this money and set up different accounts to teach your grandchildren how to invest money wisely.

You can do whatever you wish, as long as you keep in mind that you may need this account to generate income for you later on if your QRPs run out of money (like Joe and Carol's did). *This is why you need to be financially disciplined.* If you go out and spend your side account down to zero, then this type of planning can do you real harm. ***You must be disciplined.***

As long as you are financially disciplined, this is how your Golden Years become truly Golden. Nothing frees you up to do the things that make life enjoyable more than a big pot of tax-free cash!

CHAPTER 10

"IRA Tax Rescue Plan" with RMDs

*"The person who gets the farthest is generally the
one who is willing to do and dare.
The sure-thing boat never gets far from shore."*
—*Dale Carnegie*

In the last chapter, we looked at a plan that would help Joe and
Carol both reduce their taxes and increase their net worth when
they were taking their earnings out of their retirement accounts.
In this chapter, we'll look at the situation where Joe and Carol are
reinvesting, and plan on only taking out their Required Minimum
Distributions (RMDs).

Current Circumstances

Figure 10-1 details Joe and Carol's future distributions should they choose to reinvest their QRPs and only take out their required minimum distributions (RMD), again keeping all of our assumptions consistent.

In this scenario, Joe and Carol are forced to withdraw, and pay tax on $710,642. At their 30 percent marginal tax rate, this leads to a tax liability of $213,193. In addition to this tax, they are leaving their children a taxable account of $1,170,576. Again, using an admittedly low 30 percent marginal tax rate, that works out to $351,173. Let's add it up:

- Joe and Carol's tax bill: $213,193
- Children's tax bill: $351,173
- Total tax bill: **$564,366**

Let's see, a total tax bill of over $550,000 on QRPs that started out at $500,000. It sure makes you want to be the IRS, doesn't it?

In the last chapter, we introduced the IRA Tax Rescue Plan. For review, it works like this:

Figure 10-1

Age Beg. Of Year	Age End Of Year	Beginning Balance	8.00% Earnings	RMD Divisor	Amount Distributed	Taxable Balance
65	66	$500,000	$40,000		$0	$540,000
66	67	$540,000	$43,200		$0	$583,200
67	68	$583,200	$46,656		$0	$629,856
68	69	$629,856	$50,388		$0	$680,244
69	70	$680,244	$54,420		$0	$734,664
70	71	$734,664	$58,773	27.4	$26,813	$766,625
71	72	$766,625	$61,330	26.5	$28,929	$799,025
72	73	$799,025	$63,922	25.6	$31,212	$831,735
73	74	$831,735	$66,539	24.7	$33,673	$864,601
74	75	$864,601	$69,168	23.8	$36,328	$897,441
75	76	$897,441	$71,795	22.9	$39,190	$930,047
76	77	$930,047	$74,404	22.0	$42,275	$962,176
77	78	$962,176	$76,974	21.2	$45,386	$993,764
78	79	$993,764	$79,501	20.3	$48,954	$1,024,311
79	80	$1,024,311	$81,945	19.5	$52,529	$1,053,727
80	81	$1,053,727	$84,298	18.7	$56,349	$1,081,677
81	82	$1,081,677	$86,534	17.9	$60,429	$1,107,782
82	83	$1,107,782	$88,623	17.1	$64,783	$1,131,622
83	84	$1,131,622	$90,530	16.3	$69,425	$1,152,727
84	85	$1,152,727	$92,218	15.5	$74,369	$1,170,576

Total Taxable Distributions: $710,642

Hypothetical only - no specific investment illustrated.

STEP ONE: A home loan is taken out on an interest-only basis. This means that *only the interest* will be paid and NOT the principal. Why? Because interest is usually deductible on your tax return, but principal is not.

STEP TWO: Take additional distributions out of the QRP to pay the interest payment. This will normally lead to a tax-free distribution of the additional amount out of the QRP. The QRP additional distribution is normally taxable, *but it is completely offset by the deduction of the interest!* (Note: Please consult your tax advisor to determine if the interest payment would be fully deductible for you, as this may not always be the case.)

STEP THREE: Invest the proceeds from the home loan into a safe, liquid side account that offers multiple tax advantages (similar to a Roth IRA). A Maximum Funded Equity Indexed Universal Life Insurance Plan can work very well in these circumstances.

Joe and Carol have a home worth $400,000 completely paid for, so we have them take out a loan of $300,000 at a 7 percent fixed interest-only rate. To make the loan payments, we take $21,000 out of their QRPs. In this example, we are going to take additional dollars out (on top of the loan payments) and transfer the after-tax amount to the side account as well.

> Our goal is to get the money out of the QRPs during Joe and Carol's lifetime (if we can) and get that money transferred to a place that is tax-free (the side account) while paying as little tax as possible on the transition. We want Joe and Carol's money growing in a tax-free environment, not a taxable one.

Figure 10-2 shows you the impact of this planning on Joe and Carol's QRPs.

Figure 10-2

Age Beg. Of Year	Age End Of Year	Beginning Balance	8.00% Earnings	Amount Distributed	Less Home Interest	Amount Taxable	Taxable Balance
65	66	$500,000	$40,000	$60,000	$21,000	$39,000	$480,000
66	67	$480,000	$38,400	$60,000	$21,000	$39,000	$458,400
67	68	$458,400	$36,672	$60,000	$21,000	$39,000	$435,072
68	69	$435,072	$34,806	$60,000	$21,000	$39,000	$409,878
69	70	$409,878	$32,790	$60,000	$21,000	$39,000	$382,668
70	71	$382,668	$30,613	$60,000	$21,000	$39,000	$353,281
71	72	$353,281	$28,263	$60,000	$21,000	$39,000	$321,544
72	73	$321,544	$25,724	$60,000	$21,000	$39,000	$287,267
73	74	$287,267	$22,981	$60,000	$21,000	$39,000	$250,249
74	75	$250,249	$20,020	$60,000	$21,000	$39,000	$210,269
75	76	$210,269	$16,822	$60,000	$21,000	$39,000	$167,090
76	77	$167,090	$13,367	$60,000	$21,000	$39,000	$120,457
77	78	$120,457	$9,637	$60,000	$21,000	$39,000	$70,094
78	79	$70,094	$5,608	$60,000	$21,000	$39,000	$15,702
79	80	$15,702	$1,256	$16,958	$21,000	($4,042)	$0
80	81	$0	$0	$0	$21,000	($21,000)	$0
81	82	$0	$0	$0	$21,000	($21,000)	$0
82	83	$0	$0	$0	$21,000	($21,000)	$0
83	84	$0	$0	$0	$21,000	($21,000)	$0
84	85	$0	$0	$0	$21,000	($21,000)	$0
		Totals:	$356,958	$856,958	$420,000	$436,958	

Hypothetical only - no specific investment illustrated.

This works out very nicely. We are able to get all of the money out of Joe and Carol's QRPs, but only pay tax on $436,958 worth of distributions. At our 30 percent marginal tax rate, that leads to tax of $131,087. This is a much nicer number than the $564,366 we saw before!

- Previous tax bill total: $564,366
- New tax bill total: $131,087
- Tax savings from planning: $433,279

This represents a substantial tax reduction for Joe, Carol and their family approximating 80 percent!

However, just like in the last chapter, this planning comes with good news and bad news. The good news comes in the form of the tax reduction. You probably have already guessed the bad news. You're right—the QRPs are now at zero, so the children inherit nothing from those accounts. But just like in the last chapter, what do Joe and Carol have now that they did not have before? Their side account that has been safely growing!

Before we get into the specifics of that side account, let's not leave Figure 10-2 quite yet. We need to spend a few minutes on the distribution amount of $60,000 and what's happening to that money.

The first $21,000 goes to the mortgage payments, and is thereby tax-free. The balance of $39,000, however, is taxable. Again, using our 30 percent tax bracket, we get the following result:

- Gross distribution after mortgage payment: $39,000
- Less tax of 30%: $11,700
- Net after-tax distribution: $27,300

What did I say we were doing with this $27,300? That's correct—we are depositing this into our side account along with the equity we extracted from Joe and Carol's home.

So Joe and Carol's side account will include both the $300,000 from the mortgage and the $27,300 from the QRPs as long as they last. Once their QRPs are exhausted, we will take distributions from the side account to pay for the mortgage. Figure 10-3 shows the results.

Plan Results

This time the results are so good for Joe and Carol that it's almost a no-brainer. When we started this chapter, Joe, Carol and their children distributed a total over $1.8 million and paid tax every step of the way.

- Joe and Carol's taxable distributions: $710,642
- Children's taxable inheritance: $1,170,576
- Total taxable distributions: **$1,881,218**
- Less tax at 30%: $564,365
- After-tax value of total distributions: **$1,316,853**

Compare that result to the result from Figure 10-3. We see that now the side account grows to over $1.6 million, all tax-free! This is almost $300,000 more in the family's pocket just by utilizing the IRA Tax Rescue Plan.

- Net tax-free value of life insurance: $1,613,594
- After-tax value of current planning: $1,316,853
- Net benefit of planning: **$296,741**

Figure 10-3

Age Beg. Of Year	Age End Of Year	Premium	Cash Value	Surrender Value	Death Benefit	Cash Flow	Net Death Benefit
65	66	$90,900	$86,581	$38,580	$1,043,510	$0	$743,510
66	67	$90,900	$178,995	$130,994	$1,043,510	$0	$743,510
67	68	$90,900	$277,612	$229,611	$1,043,510	$0	$743,510
68	69	$90,900	$383,381	$335,380	$1,043,510	$0	$743,510
69	70	$90,900	$497,216	$449,215	$1,043,510	$0	$743,510
70	71	$27,300	$554,597	$510,916	$1,043,510	$0	$743,510
71	72	$27,300	$616,133	$576,772	$1,043,510	$0	$743,510
72	73	$27,300	$682,437	$647,396	$1,043,510	$0	$743,510
73	74	$27,300	$753,901	$723,180	$1,043,510	$0	$743,510
74	75	$27,300	$835,242	$808,841	$1,043,510	$0	$743,510
75	76	$27,300	$923,806	$902,206	$1,043,510	$0	$743,510
76	77	$27,300	$1,020,686	$1,003,405	$1,071,720	$0	$771,720
77	78	$27,300	$1,125,412	$1,112,452	$1,181,683	$0	$881,683
78	79	$27,300	$1,238,189	$1,229,549	$1,300,099	$0	$1,000,099
79	80	$0	$1,328,091	$1,323,785	$1,394,496	$4,042	$1,094,496
80	81	$0	$1,412,970	$1,412,970	$1,483,618	$14,700	$1,183,618
81	82	$0	$1,504,357	$1,504,357	$1,579,574	$14,700	$1,279,574
82	83	$0	$1,602,728	$1,602,728	$1,682,865	$14,700	$1,382,865
83	84	$0	$1,708,590	$1,708,590	$1,794,020	$14,700	$1,494,020
84	85	$0	$1,822,470	$1,822,470	$1,913,594	$14,700	$1,613,594
		$700,200				$77,542	

A typical Maximum Funded Equity Indexed Universal Life Plan - 65 year old male, good health.

And just like before, do Joe and Carol need to sit back and let the side account grow without spending any money? Of course not! Just like before, I recommend that they spend their money on anything that they feel is appropriate.

Now don't make the mistake in thinking that the death benefit is all for Joe and Carol's children! This insurance policy is very liquid. If Joe and Carol want to spend some (or all) of this money, they can. In fact, I would encourage them to spend all the money they want.

If they need or want a new car, pull the money out of the insurance plan tax-free to buy it. If they want to go on a trip to Europe or Australia (or China or South America or wherever!), pull the money out of the insurance plan tax-free to pay for it. If they want to buy another home, finance it, then take more money out of the QRPs to pay for it, and then use the insurance plan money tax-free to make the payments when their QRPs run out of money.

Joe and Carol should spend this account any way they see fit! And if they spend some of this money, what is the result to their heirs? It's very simple—the death benefit is reduced by an amount equal to what Joe and Carol spend.

What if Joe and Carol spend $500,000 of this account during their retirement years? So what—it's their money. So the children end up with $1.1 million tax-free. Before, they were getting $1.1 million taxable. They still end up with significantly more money.

Other Benefits

Some of the other benefits of this planning for Joe and Carol are too important to be ignored. Primarily, I am talking about better control of future taxation along with significantly better flexibility.

Insofar as future taxation is concerned, remember our discussion on the future of taxation in Chapter Four. Taxes are heading north, whether we want to accept this or not. By using this plan, Joe and Carol are getting money out of their QRPs now, when taxes are as low as they will ever be. If they wait, they will almost certainly pay at a higher rate, thus increasing their future taxation.

In addition, once the funds are out of the QRPs, the impact of the distribution on their Social Security income will go to zero. As a result, they have a potential future opportunity of reducing the tax on their Social Security income (although I wouldn't bet on it!).

I would argue that the more important of the other benefits has to do with Joe and Carol's enhanced flexibility. With an IRA, once you are 70½, who decides whether or not you take money out? The IRS. Who determines what your minimum distribution must be? The IRS. Who takes a cut every single time you take money out? The IRS.

But after implementing this plan, who's making all the decisions now? Now Joe and Carol are calling all the shots. They determine if and when and how much they withdraw out of their side account. The IRS has no power over them.

Joe and Carol intentionally are drawing more than they must out of their QRPs. Can the IRS stop them? Can the IRS do anything to prevent Joe and Carol from following our plan? No they can't, so once again, Joe and Carol are in the driver's seat. They are in control.

Summary

In this chapter, we used the IRA Tax Rescue Plan in a situation where Joe and Carol were planning on taking only the Required Minimum

Distribution from their QRPs. We learned that this planning program provided huge benefits in such a situation.

The IRA Tax Rescue Plan slashed the total taxation down from over $560,000 to around $130,000. That's over $400,000 of tax that Joe and Carol keep within the family versus just handing over to the IRS! Additionally, this plan significantly enhanced Joe and Carol's net worth, creating more tax-free dollars for them to spend during their lifetime to fully enjoy their Golden Years. And it left a whole bunch more money to their heirs, again 100 percent tax-free.

Anyway you look at it, this planning strategy provided Joe and Carol a huge win for them and their family, all at the cost of the IRS. Not at all a bad deal when you add it all up!

CHAPTER 11

Total Asset Deployment

"Do what you can, with what you have, where you are."
—Theodore Roosevelt

In the last two chapters, we saw how using the equity in Joe and Carol's home in a smart and creative way made a lot of sense. But Joe and Carol were already retired. Do you have to wait until then to take advantage of this type of planning?

In this chapter, we are going to learn if utilizing home equity also makes sense at younger ages. In other words, does this idea work at all ages?

Remember, at the end of Chapter Eight, we learned that the Federal Reserve Bank of Chicago published a study in August 2006 that concluded that putting dollars into tax-deferred accounts (TDA) is smarter than paying off the principal of your home. Now we're going to determine if using a TDA is the best way to invest those dollars, or if other strategies work even better.

Let's start with going back to John and Sara …

John and Sara

John and Sara, you may remember, are both thirty years old and starting to save for retirement. They are considering contributing $3,000 each into their QRPs at work. Unfortunately, their employers do not match their contributions at all. As you may remember from earlier chapters, if they follow this path for the next thirty-five years, their results might look like the chart in Figure 11-1.

From Figure 11-1, we find that John and Sara reach age sixty-five with $1,075,257 in their account, and if they took 100 percent of the income each year, it would look like this:

- $1,075,257 × 8% = $86,021
- Less 30% tax = $25,806
- Net income =   **$60,215**

Now, here's the question—could John and Sara do better by using a strategy I call Total Asset Deployment? Let's find out!

Figure 11-1

Age Beg. Of Year	Age End Of Year	Beginning Balance	Annual Contribution	Tax Savings	8.00% Earnings	Ending Balance
30	31	$0	$6,000	$1,800	$240	$6,240
31	32	$6,240	$6,000	$1,800	$739	$12,979
32	33	$12,979	$6,000	$1,800	$1,278	$20,258
33	34	$20,258	$6,000	$1,800	$1,861	$28,118
34	35	$28,118	$6,000	$1,800	$2,489	$36,608
35	36	$36,608	$6,000	$1,800	$3,169	$45,776
36	37	$45,776	$6,000	$1,800	$3,902	$55,678
37	38	$55,678	$6,000	$1,800	$4,694	$66,373
38	39	$66,373	$6,000	$1,800	$5,550	$77,922
39	40	$77,922	$6,000	$1,800	$6,474	$90,396
40	41	$90,396	$6,000	$1,800	$7,472	$103,868
41	42	$103,868	$6,000	$1,800	$8,549	$118,417
42	43	$118,417	$6,000	$1,800	$9,713	$134,131
43	44	$134,131	$6,000	$1,800	$10,970	$151,101
44	45	$151,101	$6,000	$1,800	$12,328	$169,429
45	46	$169,429	$6,000	$1,800	$13,794	$189,224
46	47	$189,224	$6,000	$1,800	$15,378	$210,601
47	48	$210,601	$6,000	$1,800	$17,088	$233,690
48	49	$233,690	$6,000	$1,800	$18,935	$258,625
49	50	$258,625	$6,000	$1,800	$20,930	$285,555
50	51	$285,555	$6,000	$1,800	$23,084	$314,639
51	52	$314,639	$6,000	$1,800	$25,411	$346,050
52	53	$346,050	$6,000	$1,800	$27,924	$379,974
53	54	$379,974	$6,000	$1,800	$30,638	$416,612
54	55	$416,612	$6,000	$1,800	$33,569	$456,181
55	56	$456,181	$6,000	$1,800	$36,734	$498,916
56	57	$498,916	$6,000	$1,800	$40,153	$545,069
57	58	$545,069	$6,000	$1,800	$43,846	$594,914
58	59	$594,914	$6,000	$1,800	$47,833	$648,747
59	60	$648,747	$6,000	$1,800	$52,140	$706,887
60	61	$706,887	$6,000	$1,800	$56,791	$769,678
61	62	$769,678	$6,000	$1,800	$61,814	$837,492
62	63	$837,492	$6,000	$1,800	$67,239	$910,732
63	64	$910,732	$6,000	$1,800	$73,099	$989,830
64	65	$989,830	$6,000	$1,800	$79,426	$1,075,257
		Totals:	$210,000	$63,000	$865,257	

Hypothetical only - no specific investment illustrated.

141

Total Asset Deployment

With Total Asset Deployment, we utilize the following strategy:

STEP ONE: Take out an interest-only loan against your home's equity. For John and Sara, we want to match a payment of $6,000 per year, so ...

$6,000/7% interest rate = $85,714 loan.

STEP TWO: Invest the proceeds from the home loan over a five-year period into a Maximum Funded Equity Indexed Life Insurance Plan.

STEP THREE: Pay the loan out of pocket *instead* of contributing to a QRP.

Based on this strategy, John and Sara receive $85,714 from the loan (I am assuming that they have enough equity in their home to do this, of course). They take $18,500 from the $85,000 to invest in the policy, and the balance gets invested in a laddered CD (or government bond or fixed annuity) portfolio to guarantee the later premiums. Figure 11-2 shows you what the results are for John and Sara.

Figure 11-2

Age Beg. Of Year	Age End Of Year	Premium	Cash Value	Surrender Value	Death Benefit	Cash Flow	Net Death Benefit
30	31	$18,500	$16,962	$7,267	$611,730	$0	$526,016
31	32	$18,500	$35,262	$26,212	$611,730	$0	$526,016
32	33	$18,500	$54,996	$46,593	$611,730	$0	$526,016
33	34	$18,500	$76,287	$68,530	$611,730	$0	$526,016
34	35	$18,500	$99,261	$92,151	$611,730	$0	$526,016
35	36	$0	$105,136	$98,672	$611,730	$0	$526,016
36	37	$0	$111,461	$105,643	$611,730	$0	$526,016
37	38	$0	$118,271	$113,100	$611,730	$0	$526,016
38	39	$0	$125,606	$121,082	$611,730	$0	$526,016
39	40	$0	$134,802	$130,923	$611,730	$0	$526,016
40	41	$0	$145,669	$142,437	$611,730	$0	$526,016
41	42	$0	$157,485	$154,899	$611,730	$0	$526,016
42	43	$0	$170,321	$168,382	$611,730	$0	$526,016
43	44	$0	$184,273	$182,980	$611,730	$0	$526,016
44	45	$0	$199,442	$198,795	$611,730	$0	$526,016
45	46	$0	$215,922	$215,922	$611,730	$0	$526,016
46	47	$0	$233,842	$233,842	$611,730	$0	$526,016
47	48	$0	$253,331	$253,331	$611,730	$0	$526,016
48	49	$0	$274,535	$274,535	$611,730	$0	$526,016
49	50	$0	$297,609	$297,609	$611,730	$0	$526,016
50	51	$0	$322,731	$322,731	$611,730	$0	$526,016
51	52	$0	$350,094	$350,094	$611,730	$0	$526,016
52	53	$0	$379,886	$379,886	$623,014	$0	$537,300
53	54	$0	$412,300	$412,300	$647,311	$0	$561,597
54	55	$0	$447,571	$447,571	$671,357	$0	$585,643
55	56	$0	$485,963	$485,963	$709,506	$0	$623,792
56	57	$0	$527,714	$527,714	$749,354	$0	$663,640
57	58	$0	$573,122	$573,122	$790,909	$0	$705,195
58	59	$0	$622,517	$622,517	$834,173	$0	$748,459
59	60	$0	$676,260	$676,260	$879,138	$0	$793,424
60	61	$0	$734,748	$734,748	$940,478	$0	$854,764
61	62	$0	$798,332	$798,332	$1,005,898	$0	$920,184
62	63	$0	$867,460	$867,460	$1,075,650	$0	$989,936
63	64	$0	$942,626	$942,626	$1,150,004	$0	$1,064,290
64	65	$0	$1,024,366	$1,024,366	$1,229,239	$0	$1,143,525
65	66	$0	$1,008,891	$1,008,891	$1,201,291	$96,000	$1,115,577
66	67	$0	$993,754	$993,754	$1,191,832	$96,000	$1,106,118
67	68	$0	$979,063	$979,063	$1,182,354	$96,000	$1,096,640
68	69	$0	$964,975	$964,975	$1,172,893	$96,000	$1,087,179
69	70	$0	$951,673	$951,673	$1,163,490	$96,000	$1,077,776
70	71	$0	$939,365	$939,365	$1,138,848	$96,000	$1,053,134
71	72	$0	$928,537	$928,537	$1,111,985	$96,000	$1,026,271
72	73	$0	$919,593	$919,593	$1,082,747	$96,000	$997,033
73	74	$0	$913,007	$913,007	$1,050,977	$96,000	$965,263
74	75	$0	$909,351	$909,351	$1,016,530	$96,000	$930,816
75	76	$0	$909,313	$909,313	$1,025,914	$96,000	$940,200
76	77	$0	$912,570	$912,570	$1,039,413	$96,000	$953,699
77	78	$0	$919,589	$919,589	$1,057,562	$96,000	$971,848
78	79	$0	$930,879	$930,879	$1,080,945	$96,000	$995,231
79	80	$0	$947,002	$947,002	$1,110,205	$96,000	$1,024,491
80	81	$0	$968,568	$968,568	$1,146,036	$96,000	$1,060,322
81	82	$0	$996,244	$996,244	$1,189,200	$96,000	$1,103,486
82	83	$0	$1,030,765	$1,030,765	$1,240,533	$96,000	$1,154,819
83	84	$0	$1,072,926	$1,072,926	$1,300,936	$96,000	$1,215,222
84	85	$0	$1,123,554	$1,123,554	$1,371,350	$96,000	$1,285,636
		$92,500				$1,920,000	

A typical Maximum Funded Equity Indexed Universal Life Plan - Male age 30, good health.

143

This strategy results in an annual retirement income of $96,000 per year for John and Sara (tax-free!), but we can't forget that they still need to pay $6,000 toward their annual home loan interest. So John and Sara net out $90,000 of income versus $60,000.

- Net income after planning: $90,000
- Net income before planning: $60,215
- Benefit from planning: **$29,785**

This represents an improvement of almost 50 percent more money each year in retirement simply by using leverage and being smart and creative with investment dollars. Over a twenty-year retirement, John and Sara will receive approximately $600,000 more income with this plan versus traditional planning. And instead of leaving their children $1,075,257 in taxable accounts, they leave them $1,285,636 in a tax-free death benefit. This is huge!

In addition, their income is now tax-free and does NOT impact any future Social Security income they may receive. They have complete freedom to determine if, when and how much money they desire to take out and spend in addition to their $96,000 of income.

Another benefit comes in the form of college planning. John and Sara do not have to wait until age 59½ to take money out of this plan. They can take money out at any age. So if they want to use some of their account funds for college for their children, they can. Plus, this account is completely invisible to the financial aid calculations for college.

All told, the Total Asset Deployment Plan is a huge win for John and Sara, and any children that they may have. Wouldn't life be a lot easier if every decision was this simple?

Total Asset Deployment for a Fifty-Year-Old Couple

"That's great," you say, but maybe you aren't thirty years old. Maybe you're more like fifty. Would this approach also work for someone your age? Again, an example may help.

Bob and Mary Smith are both fifty years old. Due to various reasons, they've determined that it's time to finally get serious about their retirement planning. After looking at their budget, they've determined that they can save another $500/month, and they're trying to figure out the best place to invest that money.

Bob and Mary's financial situation follows:

- Home value: $475,000
- Mortgage: $150,000 balance, payments = $1,200/month
- Auto loan: $20,000 balance, payments = $400/month
- Credit cards: $10,000 balance, payments = $200/month*

Note: Bob and Mary pay an extra $100/month on the credit cards.

Total Debt: $180,000
Total Monthly Payments: $1,900/month

The first thing we should do is identify the value of investing the $500 per month into a QRP. Figure 11-3 outlines this approach, using all of the same assumptions we've been making throughout the book.

As you can see, Bob and Mary have an account that has grown to $169,429, and the income generated is calculated below:

- $169,429 × 8% earnings = $13,554
- Less 30% tax = $4,066
- Net income =   **$9,488**

Figure 11-3

Age Beg. Of Year	Age End Of Year	Beginning Balance	Annual Investment	8.00% Earnings	Ending Balance
50	51	$0	$6,000	$240	**$6,240**
51	52	$6,240	$6,000	$739	**$12,979**
52	53	$12,979	$6,000	$1,278	**$20,258**
53	54	$20,258	$6,000	$1,861	**$28,118**
54	55	$28,118	$6,000	$2,489	**$36,608**
55	56	$36,608	$6,000	$3,169	**$45,776**
56	57	$45,776	$6,000	$3,902	**$55,678**
57	58	$55,678	$6,000	$4,694	**$66,373**
58	59	$66,373	$6,000	$5,550	**$77,922**
59	60	$77,922	$6,000	$6,474	**$90,396**
60	61	$90,396	$6,000	$7,472	**$103,868**
61	62	$103,868	$6,000	$8,549	**$118,417**
62	63	$118,417	$6,000	$9,713	**$134,131**
63	64	$134,131	$6,000	$10,970	**$151,101**
64	65	$151,101	$6,000	$12,328	**$169,429**
		Totals:	**$90,000**	**$79,429**	

Hypothetical only - no specific investment illustrated.

Now that we've calculated this result, let's see how the Total Asset Deployment strategy could work for Bob and Mary ...

Total Asset Deployment—Bob and Mary

Again, the strategy works as follows:

STEP ONE: Take out an interest-only loan against your home's equity.

STEP TWO: Invest the proceeds from the home loan over a five-year period into a Maximum Funded Equity Indexed Life Insurance Plan.

STEP THREE: Pay the loan out of pocket *instead* of contributing to a QRP.

From above, the current total debt is $180,000 and the total payments are $1,900 per month. Let's assume that we refinance the home and pay off all debt. How much can we refinance?

- $1,900 current payment × 12 months = $22,800
- Additional $500 per month × 12 months = $6,000
- Total potential annual mortgage payment =   **$28,800**

147

In order to calculate the size of their potential mortgage, we need to assume an interest rate. Let's assume an interest-only loan at a fifteen-year fixed rate at 7 percent.

- $28,800 payment/7% interest rate = $411,429
- Less current debt = $180,000
- Net equity employed =   **$231,429**

Bob and Mary invest $50,000 of the $231,429 into a Maximum Funded Equity Indexed Life Insurance plan on Bob's life. This represents the first year premium. The other $181,429 goes into a laddered CD (or government bond or fixed annuity) portfolio that guarantees the premiums for the later years. Figure 11-4 shows you how that plan works out.

Now we see that Bob and Mary receive income of $50,000 per year, but again, we need to remember that they have to make the mortgage payment of $28,800. So they net out $21,200 per year of annual income—more than double the $9,488 they were getting from investing in a QRP!

- Net income after planning: $21,200
- Net income before planning: $9,488
- Annual benefit from planning: **$11,712**

If Bob and Mary live twenty years in retirement, then they have over $230,000 more to spend thanks to planning versus doing what everyone else does (the QRP route). In addition, the income from

Figure 11-4

Age Beg. Of Year	Age End Of Year	Premium	Cash Value	Surrender Value	Death Benefit	Cash Flow	Net Death Benefit
50	51	$50,000	$48,871	$30,655	$841,406	$0	$429,977
51	52	$50,000	$101,498	$83,282	$841,406	$0	$429,977
52	53	$50,000	$158,223	$140,007	$841,406	$0	$429,977
53	54	$50,000	$219,422	$201,206	$841,406	$0	$429,977
54	55	$50,000	$285,451	$267,235	$841,406	$0	$429,977
55	56	$0	$305,489	$288,912	$841,406	$0	$429,977
56	57	$0	$327,050	$312,113	$841,406	$0	$429,977
57	58	$0	$350,270	$336,972	$841,406	$0	$429,977
58	59	$0	$375,270	$363,612	$841,406	$0	$429,977
59	60	$0	$404,142	$394,123	$841,406	$0	$429,977
60	61	$0	$435,342	$427,145	$841,406	$0	$429,977
61	62	$0	$469,119	$462,561	$841,406	$0	$429,977
62	63	$0	$505,735	$500,817	$841,406	$0	$429,977
63	64	$0	$545,483	$542,204	$841,406	$0	$429,977
64	65	$0	$588,676	$587,036	$841,406	$0	$429,977
65	66	$0	$581,925	$581,925	$787,930	$50,000	$376,501
66	67	$0	$575,636	$575,636	$730,737	$50,000	$319,308
67	68	$0	$569,951	$569,951	$696,055	$50,000	$284,626
68	69	$0	$564,696	$564,696	$693,009	$50,000	$281,580
69	70	$0	$559,884	$559,884	$689,951	$50,000	$278,522
70	71	$0	$555,613	$555,613	$677,511	$50,000	$266,082
71	72	$0	$552,113	$552,113	$663,677	$50,000	$252,248
72	73	$0	$549,570	$549,570	$648,324	$50,000	$236,895
73	74	$0	$548,203	$548,203	$631,325	$50,000	$219,896
74	75	$0	$548,275	$548,275	$612,547	$50,000	$201,118
75	76	$0	$550,097	$550,097	$619,696	$50,000	$208,267
76	77	$0	$553,514	$553,514	$628,885	$50,000	$217,456
77	78	$0	$558,738	$558,738	$640,360	$50,000	$228,931
78	79	$0	$566,000	$566,000	$654,390	$50,000	$242,961
79	80	$0	$575,550	$575,550	$671,269	$50,000	$259,840
80	81	$0	$587,664	$587,664	$691,316	$50,000	$279,887
81	82	$0	$602,640	$602,640	$714,878	$50,000	$303,449
82	83	$0	$620,807	$620,807	$742,335	$50,000	$330,906
83	84	$0	$642,519	$642,519	$774,097	$50,000	$362,668
84	85	$0	$668,143	$668,143	$810,589	$50,000	$399,160

$250,000 $1,000,000

A typical Maximum Funded Equity Indexed Universal Life Plan - Male age 50, good health.

the insurance pays 100 percent of their mortgage payment for them, so it's like their home is paid for. Also, their tax-free death benefit of $399,160 after paying off the mortgage in full ($411,429) is much larger for their children than the taxable QRP worth $169,429.

Remember, the insurance pays Bob and Mary tax-free income, which does NOT affect their Social Security income. Also, they still get to use the tax deduction of the mortgage interest during their retirement to offset any other income. Finally, they are able to pay off both their cars and credit cards—a nice bonus.

When all is said and done, the Total Asset Deployment program ends up providing significantly more value than a Qualified Retirement Plan for Bob and Mary. But what expert would have ever recommended this to them?

Summary

The Total Asset Deployment program combines two actions that fly against all so-called "common-sense" thinking. It utilizes a loan to take equity out of your home and invests that equity into a Maximum Funded Equity Indexed Life Insurance Plan. Who would ever consider doing such a crazy thing?

Yet, when you run the numbers, when this program is done properly and in the right circumstances, you can often end up with significant increases in retirement income, while maintaining a tax deduction (home interest) that can be used to offset other income from pensions, Social Security, and the like. Your age turns out to be unimportant. This program works at almost any age!

CHAPTER 12

Other Options

"The secret of success in life is for a man to be ready for
his opportunity when it comes."
—*Benjamin Disraeli*

In this chapter, we will look at some additional strategies that can be utilized to extract money out of your QRPs without taxation. Some of these strategies can be used by anyone, but a couple are reserved for "Accredited Investors."

Accredited Investors are defined as someone who either: a) has a net worth exceeding $1 million, or b) has earned more than $200,000 for at least the last two years and expects to do so again this year. We'll start with the strategies that anyone can use.

Charitable Planning

One of the interesting things about the tax code is that charitable planning offers so many benefits that someone who is not charitably inclined may decide to become so. The bad news is that financial planners have come up with so many creative strategies in this area that it can become confusing.

Rather than try to cover every single type of charitable strategy that might be helpful, I'll focus on the one that seems to be used the most often—the Charitable Remainder Trust (CRT).

Charitable Remainder Trusts (CRT)

The concept of a CRT is not complex. In fact, it is relatively simple to understand. With a CRT, you are gifting assets (non-retirement plan assets) to a charitable trust that will be given to your selected charities after you (and your spouse) die. The assets are sold within the trust tax-free and are invested in such a manner that they provide you income for your (and your spouse's) lifetime.

If you are a visual learner (like me), it looks like the chart on the following page.

You enjoy some nice benefits from this type of planning. First, you receive a sizable tax deduction for your gift to the charitable trust. Now you don't receive a tax deduction equal to 100 percent of the gift, because you are not giving it to the charity today, you are making a "future gift." In other words, the charity gets the money

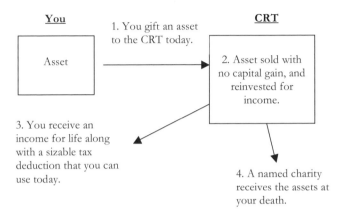

after you (and your spouse) die. So the IRS discounts the value of your gift to take this into account. For example, if you are gifting $1 million, you might receive a deduction of $300,000 to $600,000 depending on your age and the amount of income you take.

What could you do with this tax deduction?
How about using it to convert a chunk of your QRP to a Roth IRA tax-free?

Second, you receive income for your lifetime, provided the assets in the CRT last. For this reason, you must invest wisely inside the CRT. Third, this strategy allows you to sell an appreciated asset *without paying capital gains tax.* Why? Because charities are tax exempt and don't pay capital gains, and a CRT enjoys the same tax treatment.

So let's assume that you have a piece of property that has appreciated nicely. You want to sell it and invest the proceeds for income, but if you sell, you'll owe a big capital gain tax. This strategy can help you out. Or what if you have a stock that has appreciated over the years, and you want to sell, but you don't want to pay the capital gains tax. Same thing—use a CRT.

CRT Problems

So far, it probably sounds like this CRT strategy is the ultimate win for you at the IRS's expense. And it pretty much is, with one exception. If you are paying close attention, you are probably waving your hand right now saying, "Wait a minute here! If the asset goes to the charity at death, what happens to my children and/or grandchildren? Don't they lose out?"

Good job—you are paying attention! You are exactly right! Assets that are gifted to a CRT are taken out of the family. At your death, that money goes to the charity and not to your family. Now that may be OK in some situations, but most people would prefer to see their assets stay within the family. Does this mean your can't use a CRT if you want your assets to stay within the family? Of course not, because we can easily fix that problem.

Let's go back to our CRT example and add another piece:

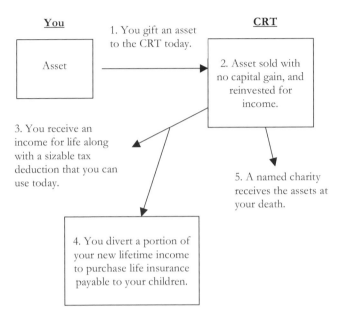

All I'm doing here is taking a portion of the lifetime income you receive and redirecting it to an insurance plan that pays off after you (and your spouse) die. This way, not only does the charity receive the asset value at your death, but so does your family, and it's *all tax-free!* Who's the big loser now? The IRS! And we don't care if they find themselves on the short end of the stick for once, do we?

The CRT does have two more disadvantages. The first may be a large disadvantage, but maybe not. Assets transferred into a CRT are NOT liquid. What does that mean? It means that you CANNOT take out lump sums from the CRT—only income. In essence, you are trading your asset for an income stream for life, very similar to a traditional income annuity. That asset is now gone, except for the income.

The second disadvantage is that you give up a measure of control over that asset. You are giving the asset to a CRT. That means that the asset is owned and managed by the CRT and the trustee of the CRT. And you cannot be the trustee. Now many people get around that by naming a trustee who will do whatever they tell them to, but this is where you need a good attorney to write the trust.

And that brings up the final disadvantages to a CRT—you have to pay an attorney to write the trust, and then you have to file a tax return on the trust each year, which may require paying a tax preparer a little more money each year.

Overall, when you compare the huge benefits of a CRT with the usually minor downsides, this strategy can often be a big win for you and your family. And remember, this is just one of dozens of charitable strategies.

Non-QRP Deferred Annuity Losses

This one appeared on the scene thanks to the stock market losses of 2000–2002. When you invest in a deferred annuity for non-retirement accounts, you enjoy tax-deferral. However, when you withdraw the money down the road, you pay income tax rates, not capital gain tax rates (which are lower).

But what if you invested $500,000, and now your account is worth $300,000? If you cash it in, you don't have any gains, you have losses. And the IRS doesn't let you claim a capital loss on these accounts. But they will let you claim an income loss up to the amount of income you have for the year.

So, if you have a $200,000 loss in your deferred annuity, you can surrender the annuity and use the loss to *convert $200,000 of your QRP to a Roth IRA without owing any tax!* This makes your loss a little bit easier to swallow.

Now, you have to be careful not to mess this one up. *You must surrender the contract and receive the cash.* Transferring the account from one company to another will NOT provide you the tax deduction. I repeat—you must receive the cash! Once you have the cash, you can start a new contract if you desire with another company.

Accredited Investor Strategies

I'm not going to go into much detail in this section, but I will hit a couple of high spots. Accredited investors, which generally means you have a net worth exceeding $1 million, have available some investment options that the rest of the population does not. And several of these options have some interesting tax benefits.

Direct Oil/Gas Investment Programs

Accredited Investors can choose to invest in partnerships that drill for oil and natural gas. These partnerships can range from highly risky exploration to relatively safer development programs.

One of the benefits that these partnerships offer (other than tax-advantaged income) is that you can often receive a substantial tax deduction, normally 70 to 100 percent, depending on the program, of your investment. Let's see how this might help get money out of a QRP tax-free.

Suppose that you have $1 million in your QRP, and for diversification purposes, you want to hold 5 percent of your portfolio in an oil/natural gas position. You could buy a mutual fund or exchange traded fund within your QRP, or maybe some stock of companies with operations in that sector of the economy. But you would almost certainly be better off using one of these direct oil/gas programs.

You take $50,000 out of your QRP (taxable) and invest it into one of these programs. You get an immediate income tax deduction between $35,000 (70 percent) and $50,000 (100 percent). So you end up paying tax on a small portion, if any, of your distribution. Meanwhile, you successfully diversify your portfolio outside of the taxable environment of the QRP and your income from the partnership is partially tax-free due to something called "depletion allowance."

As you can imagine, there are a number of disadvantages to these programs. You should investigate the pros and cons carefully before investing any money in one of them.

Tax Credit Programs

These are becoming harder to find, but section 42 of the tax code allows "Tax Credits Programs" for Accredited Investors. These programs generally invest in low-income housing, usually for retirees. They provide the investor an annual tax credit in lieu of annual income.

Each year, the investor receives a form K-1 that tells them how much of an annual credit they will receive. The maximum is normally 10 percent of the investment. For example, let's assume that you invest $60,000 into one of these programs. Each year, you receive a tax credit (instead of income) of $6,000. You take $20,000 out of your QRP, or you convert $20,000 into a Roth IRA. Either way, you will owe tax on a $20,000 distribution. At our 30 percent tax rate, you owe $6,000 of tax.

> A tax credit reduces your tax liability *dollar for dollar.* This is very different from a tax deduction. A tax deduction reduces the amount of income you pay tax on. A tax credit reduces the tax liability directly.

What does this mean? If you have a tax deduction of $6,000, your taxes are reduced by 30 percent of that number, or by $1,800. If you have a tax credit of $6,000, your taxes are reduced by $6,000.

Now, back to our example. You owe $6,000 of tax, but thanks to your tax credit program, you have a $6,000 tax credit. How much tax do you owe on that $20,000 distribution/conversion? That's right—nothing. Now what if this program gave you the $6,000 credit for the next ten years? You would be able to either distribute and spend, or convert to a Roth IRA, $200,000 with no tax.

Normally, these tax credit programs sell the real estate once the credits are used up and return your investment (and hopefully some small gains) to you. These programs also have a number of downsides (like the oil/gas) and you need to investigate them closely before investing any money.

Summary

We briefly touched on several additional techniques that you can use to extract dollars out of your QRPs without paying tax. Some of these techniques are available to everyone, like charitable planning, and others are reserved for Accredited Investors.

Please remember that you should NOT do anything without having a qualified financial advisor who understands your circumstances and is trained in tax planning on your side. In our next (and final) chapter, we're going to discuss how you can determine if the advisor you are working with now has the training and capacity to help you analyze whether the strategies in this book are appropriate for your circumstances.

Obviously, if they are not, then we'll give you some direction as to how you can find someone who does have the proper training and expertise.

CHAPTER 13

Selecting the Right Advisor

"Ye shall know the truth, and the truth shall make you free."
—New Testament, John, 8:13

This book has focused on a new and different perspective, a fresh way to think about retirement planning. Many of the concepts we discussed fly directly in the face of "normal" or "traditional" thinking. Yet the truth is the truth, even if "everyone" wishes otherwise.

You are now faced with a choice. You can take this book and put it on the shelf. You can then think to yourself, "Wow, I never really thought of retirement planning that way—I should visit my advisor about this," and then end up doing nothing. *Or you can take action.*

Nothing in this world ever happened because somebody just thought about things. Everything in this world happens because **someone takes action**.

Now don't get me wrong! I'm not telling you to go out and take action on the concepts we discussed in this book blindly. I am telling you that you should pick up the phone and schedule a meeting with your current, most trusted financial advisor (whether that be a CPA, Certified Financial Planner™, etc.) to review the concepts discussed in this book, to learn if they would be appropriate for you.

Identifying if Your Current Advisor Can Help You with These Concepts

It's sad, but true—many financial advisors (especially CPAs) are close-minded about what they consider to be new ideas. They reject out of hand any planning strategy that hasn't been done before. And if the financial magazines don't trumpet a strategy as "smart planning," then clearly (in their opinion) it should be dismissed, and any analysis is just a waste of time.

You know all about this mindset. It's the mindset of those who believed the world was flat, and Christopher Columbus was definitely going to sail off of the edge. It's the same mindset that tells us, "Man will never fly." It's the mindset that argues that pretty much anything can't be done, because it's never been done in the past.

Please do yourself a favor if you learn that your current advisor suffers from this dangerous mindset—get a new advisor! They aren't helping you, they are holding you back.

Other advisors, on the other hand, are very open to new ideas and creative strategies. They have only one concern—does this strategy make sense for your unique circumstances? Now this is the kind of advisor you want helping you to determine if the strategies in this book make sense for you. You want someone with an open mind.

But just because they have the right mindset does not mean that they are the right person! The best advisor for you needs to be able to fulfill certain vital criteria to be the right person for you.

The "Right Stuff"

The following list represents characteristics that a *Great* Financial Advisor will have, and you don't deserve anything less!

- Open-minded to new ideas—so open minded that they are constantly looking for new and better planning strategies to better serve the diverse needs of their clients.
- Ongoing education—just like doctors have to continue their education throughout their entire careers to stay on top of new techniques, so does a Great Financial Advisor. You'll know if you have this type of person already because you have called his/her office, only to learn that he/she is away at a conference or retreat.

- They call you from time to time wanting to discuss a new planning strategy that may have merit for your circumstances. They may even give you, or recommend to you, a good book to expand your thinking.

- When you bring them questions about potential new planning strategies, they consider them fully, to determine the value of the strategy for your unique situation. They certainly do NOT dismiss any strategy without evaluating its merits.

- You are comfortable meeting with them. You work together on an even level with mutual respect. You feel like you can tell them anything because they understand you and what you are all about.

- You know in your heart that you and your needs are more important to them than your portfolio. While your money is important, your goals and dreams are much more important. They know this and support you.

- You know how they are compensated. In a world of hidden fees and costs, they are upfront about how they are paid. They hide nothing.

- Most importantly, you feel that you have the "right" person to assist you with your planning. Don't neglect or discount your gut feeling about a person—it's usually right on target!

Warning Signs

Just like there are certain things to look for when evaluating your current (or a new) advisor on a positive scale, you do need to watch out for certain warning signs. Here is a list of some of the most common ones:

- Anything said or done that may violate one of the characteristics of a Great Financial Advisor listed above.

- If the advisor works *for* a brokerage house (Merrill Lynch, Smith Barney, Morgan Stanley, etc.) or *for* an insurance company (New York Life, Northwestern Mutual, MetLife, etc.), you want to be careful. **They may still be the "right" person!** However, you need to realize that these advisors almost always have limitations on what they can and cannot do. **These limitations are dictated by their home office.** And how much does a home office know about *you*? As a result, while a particular planning strategy may hold considerable merit for you and your unique circumstances, an advisor with one of these organizations may not be able to help you due to home office driven constraints. And even if they can help you, their home office may not allow them (for various reasons that have nothing to do with you) to use the optimum financial products for a particular strategy. So be careful when dealing with someone who is not independent.

- CPAs are notorious for rejecting new strategies without any consideration. Please be aware that for 95 percent of CPAs (or more), their job is to make certain that the right numbers go in the right place on your tax return. They are not financial advisors.

  - Think about this one for a moment—when do you see your CPA? If you are like most people, it's once per year during tax season. How much time do they have to do any planning for you then?

  - **Here's how you know if you have a CPA who is also truly a financial advisor—do they call you after tax season to come in for planning?** If you only see your CPA during tax season, I'm sorry to tell you that you have a tax *preparer*, not an advisor.

- If your advisor comes to your home versus you going to their office, odds are high that you have a financial salesperson, NOT a financial advisor.

  - Think about it this way—do you go to see your doctor? What about your dentist? Accountant? Attorney? Can we agree that a Great Financial Advisor is as valuable to you, if not more, than many other professionals? If not, then you haven't met one, and you don't have one!

Finding a Great Financial Advisor

Let's assume that you are reading this and thinking to yourself, "My current advisor is obviously not what I need!" Or maybe you don't have a financial advisor at all. Maybe you do everything yourself.

I hate to break it to you if you are a do-it-yourselfer, but the strategies we are discussing in this book are not ones that you want to be messing around with on your own. The tax code and insurance plans are just too complex. Managing your portfolio is one thing. These strategies are completely different.

So how do you find a Great Financial Advisor if you don't have one already? It's not always easy, but here are some ideas:

- In the yellow pages, look up "financial planning" and try to find companies that are independent. Usually (not always!) if someone is really good at financial planning, they have their own company.
- Look for the credential "CFP®," which stands for Certified Financial Planner™. Just because someone is a CFP® *does not mean* that they are automatically a Great Financial Advisor. It *does mean* that they take their education seriously. That being said, some of the most creative and best financial advisors in this country do not have their CFP® designation.
- **IMPORTANT QUESTION:** As a test, ask the potential advisor you are talking to for client references. *This is a*

167

great "trick" question! If they are willing to give you client references—stay away. I know this seems like backward thinking, but in the financial industry, with privacy rules so tight, the best advisors are *prohibited by law* to give testimonials of any kind.

- Question: Would you ask a lawyer or doctor for client references? Of course not, due to confidentiality. So why would you ask a financial advisor for them when *the best financial advisors have the same confidentiality rules as a doctor or lawyer?* I know that the magazines tell you to ask for references, but this is an area that the magazine writers are still a little behind on.

- Ask them what books they've been giving to their clients lately. This is a good question, because the Great Financial Advisors often give, and recommend, books to their clients to help expand everyone's thinking.

- **KEY QUESTION:** Ask them what strategies they've been using lately to help their clients get money out of their retirement plans without tax. Or you can ask them what their typical client's biggest tax problem is, and what they are doing to address it.

Once you've had the opportunity to find two or three who have provided acceptable answers, you need to go visit them face-to-face. Just tell them that you are looking for a new financial advisor and you are interviewing several to find the best fit. Don't be surprised if some of them send you a confidential questionnaire to fill out prior to meeting with them. They aren't being nosy, it's just part of their process.

Others may want to just sit down prior to having you fill out a questionnaire, it just depends on their process. Neither is right or wrong.

Get a feel for their office. Talk to them. Learn about their staff. How big is it? Who would you work with in the firm? Do they treat you with respect? Watch out for anyone who tries to rush you through their process. You are looking to create a long-term relationship that will be vitally important to you over time. There is no need to rush.

That being said, there is also no need to procrastinate either. Usually, after three to four meetings, you should be able to determine the firm that you want to work with. Once you've made your decision—go!

But make sure it's the right fit. If you interview two or three firms, and you are still unsure, then you haven't found the right fit. Start your process over again until you know that you have the right person for you.

Wrap Up

My purpose with this book was to help you gain a broader (and different) perspective on retirement planning. I hope that I have succeeded. You deserve to enjoy a retirement free of monetary concerns.

You should not have to worry about money because the IRS has its sticky fingers in your pocket.

You have the opportunity to take advantage of creative planning that will free you of government taxation to a great degree. Take action! Visit with your advisor, or find a new one if necessary. Be proactive, plan appropriately, and enjoy your retirement years to the fullest extent possible.

Your future is in your hands. You can either take it as it comes, or shape it as you like. You decide. You determine your future.

It's been said that the legacy we leave is a reflection of the people we touch in a positive way. By getting the IRS out of your pocket, you significantly increase the resources that you have to touch people positively. Take advantage of that, and make a difference! Live your life to the fullest extent possible, and make your Golden Years truly golden.

Appendix A
Contribution Limits - 2007

Plan Type	Under Age 50	Age 50 & Over
IRA (Traditional or Roth)	$4,000	$5,000
401(k), 403(b), 457	$15,500	$20,500
SIMPLE IRA	$10,500	$13,000

Appendix B
Uniform Distribution Table

Use for the Minimum Required Distributions during the owner's life. Do not use if the IRA owner has a spouse more than 10 years younger. Instead, use the Joint Life Table from IRS Pub. 590-SUPP.

Age of the IRA Owner	Applicable Divisor	Equivalent Percentage
70	27.4	3.65%
71	26.5	3.77%
72	25.6	3.91%
73	24.7	4.05%
74	23.8	4.20%
75	22.9	4.37%
76	22.0	4.55%
77	21.2	4.72%
78	20.3	4.93%
79	19.5	5.13%
80	18.7	5.35%
81	17.9	5.59%
82	17.1	5.85%
83	16.3	6.13%
84	15.5	6.45%
85	14.8	6.76%
86	14.1	7.09%
87	13.4	7.46%
88	12.7	7.87%
89	12.0	8.33%
90	11.4	8.77%
91	10.8	9.26%
92	10.2	9.80%
93	9.6	10.42%
94	9.1	10.99%
95	8.6	11.63%
96	8.1	12.35%
97	7.6	13.16%
98	7.1	14.08%
99	6.7	14.93%
100	6.3	15.87%
101	5.9	16.95%
102	5.5	18.18%
103	5.2	19.23%
104	4.9	20.41%
105	4.5	22.22%
106	4.2	23.81%
107	3.9	25.64%
108	3.7	27.03%
109	3.4	29.41%
110	3.1	32.26%
111	2.9	34.48%
112	2.6	38.46%
113	2.4	41.67%
114	2.1	47.62%
115 and older	1.9	52.63%

Appendix C
Single Life Expectancy Table for Inherited IRAs

Designated beneficiaries use this table based on their age in the year after the IRA owner's death. The divisor is reduced by "1" each year after the first year of distribution.

Age of the IRA Beneficiary	Applicable Divisor	Equivalent Percentage	Age of the IRA Beneficiary	Applicable Divisor	Equivalent Percentage
0	82.4	1.21%	56	28.7	3.48%
1	81.6	1.23%	57	27.9	3.58%
2	80.6	1.24%	58	27.0	3.70%
3	79.7	1.25%	59	26.1	3.83%
4	78.7	1.27%	60	25.2	3.97%
5	77.7	1.29%	61	24.4	4.10%
6	76.7	1.30%	62	23.5	4.26%
7	75.8	1.32%	63	22.7	4.41%
8	74.8	1.34%	64	21.8	4.59%
9	73.8	1.36%	65	21.0	4.76%
10	72.8	1.37%	66	20.2	4.95%
11	71.8	1.39%	67	19.4	5.15%
12	70.8	1.41%	68	18.6	5.38%
13	69.9	1.43%	69	17.8	5.62%
14	68.9	1.45%	70	17.0	5.88%
15	67.9	1.47%	71	16.3	6.13%
16	66.9	1.49%	72	15.5	6.45%
17	66.0	1.52%	73	14.8	6.76%
18	65.0	1.54%	74	14.1	7.09%
19	64.0	1.56%	75	13.4	7.46%
20	63.0	1.59%	76	12.7	7.87%
21	62.1	1.61%	77	12.1	8.26%
22	61.1	1.64%	78	11.4	8.77%
23	60.1	1.66%	79	10.8	9.26%
24	59.1	1.69%	80	10.2	9.80%
25	58.2	1.72%	81	9.7	10.31%
26	57.2	1.75%	82	9.1	10.99%
27	56.2	1.78%	83	8.6	11.63%
28	55.3	1.81%	84	8.1	12.35%
29	54.3	1.84%	85	7.6	13.16%
30	53.3	1.88%	86	7.1	14.08%
31	52.4	1.91%	87	6.7	14.93%
32	51.4	1.95%	88	6.3	15.87%
33	50.4	1.98%	89	5.9	16.95%
34	49.4	2.02%	90	5.5	18.18%
35	48.5	2.06%	91	5.2	19.23%
36	47.5	2.11%	92	4.9	20.41%
37	46.5	2.15%	93	4.6	21.74%
38	45.6	2.19%	94	4.3	23.26%
39	44.6	2.24%	95	4.1	24.39%
40	43.6	2.29%	96	3.8	26.32%
41	42.7	2.34%	97	3.6	27.78%
42	41.7	2.40%	98	3.4	29.41%
43	40.7	2.46%	99	3.1	32.26%
44	39.8	2.51%	100	2.9	34.48%
45	38.8	2.58%	101	2.7	37.04%
46	37.9	2.64%	102	2.5	40.00%
47	37.0	2.70%	103	2.3	43.48%
48	36.0	2.78%	104	2.1	47.62%
49	35.1	2.85%	105	1.9	52.63%
50	34.2	2.92%	106	1.7	58.82%
51	33.3	3.00%	107	1.5	66.67%
52	32.3	3.10%	108	1.4	71.43%
53	31.4	3.18%	109	1.2	83.33%
54	30.5	3.28%	110	1.1	90.91%
55	29.6	3.38%	111 or older	1.0	100.00%